Atlanta Braves IQ:
The Ultimate Test of True Fandom

IQ Series books are the trademark of Black Mesa Publishing, LLC.

Cataloging-in-Publication Data is available from the Library of Congress.

ISBN: 1448663210
First edition, first printing

Cover photo courtesy of author.

Black Mesa Publishing, LLC
Florida
David Horne and Marc CB Maxwell
Black.Mesa.Publishing@gmail.com

Contents

Introduction

THINK YOU KNOW BRAVES BASEBALL? Think again. In this brand new book in the IQ Sports Series find out how smart you really are about the Atlanta Braves. Are you a rookie? Are you a tested, hardcore veteran? Or will you be clearing waivers for your pending release halfway through the book?

We'll let you know.

Test your skills. Wrack your brain. It's the ultimate Atlanta Braves IQ test.

Five chapters, more than 250 questions—that's what you're up against, and we're keeping score.

Think of chapter one as Spring Training, that magical time of year when everything just feels so right with the world . . . and, when everybody, even the veterans, gets back to the basics. That's what you will find in the first chapter—50-plus questions every Braves fan should know, five each in ten different categories:

- The Numbers Game
- The Rookies
- The Veterans
- The Legends
- The Hitters
- The Pitchers
- The Managers and Coaches
- The Fabulous Feats
- The Teams
- Miscellaneous

In chapter two the season is underway and you're expected to be in shape and ready to play, so be sure and fine tune your mad trivia skills in the first chapter, because when the big club breaks camp the last thing you want is to be left behind with the rookies. The categories are the same but the questions are tougher, and the standings count.

In chapter three find out if you make the All-Star team. You have to start the season strong and then maintain a high level of consistency if you want to be on our All-Star team—and chapter three will toss the wannabes like chaff in the wind.

In chapter four it's the Dog Days of August. Can you make a push for the postseason or are you going to succumb to the pressure, unable to close the deal? We amp it up even more, and when the dust settles we'll let you know if you're deserving of chapter five.

You have to earn your way to chapter five. This is the postseason. This is where you will find trivia befitting a world champion. This is where legends are made. This is your Braves IQ, the Ultimate Test of True Fandom.

Chapter One

Spring Training

THIS IS SPRING TRAINING mind you. We're only stretching here. Just trying to get limber after a long winter of chips, couches, remote controls, beverages of choice, and the NFL . . . I mean, there's no sense straining a groin or anything else right out of the box. So we'll just start with the basics. The legends honored by the Braves with a retired jersey number. No point in sweating bullets over these questions. You don't know these, well, you don't know jack.

The Numbers Game

QUESTION 1: Dale Murphy was drafted by the Braves as the #5 overall pick in 1974, and he was originally signed as a catcher. In 2000, he was inducted into the Braves Hall of Fame. What jersey number is retired in honor of the legendary outfielder?

QUESTION 2: Warren Spahn signed out of high school for $150 and made his debut for the Braves in 1942. He won more games than any other left-handed pitcher in history and is a member of the Baseball Hall of Fame. What jersey number is retired in honor of the legendary pitcher?

QUESTION 3: It took Phil Niekro six years to reach the majors after signing as a free agent in 1958, but after making it to Milwaukee in 1964 he steadily set his career on the path to Cooperstown and baseball immortality. What jersey number is retired in honor of the legendary knuckleballer?

QUESTION 4: He signed as a 17-year-old kid and three years later Eddie Mathews was starting at third base for the Braves.

Inducted into the Hall of Fame in 1978, what jersey number is retired in honor of the legendary slugger?

QUESTION 5: The Hammer, The True Home Run Champion—nothing else needs saying, just tell us . . . what jersey number is retired in honor of Hank Aaron?

BONUS QUESTION: On July 17, 2009, the Braves honored Greg Maddux by retiring his jersey number and inducting him into the Braves Hall of Fame. This is so easy, right? What number did Maddux wear for the Braves?

BONUS QUESTION: This is one that every fan of the game should know regardless of where your loyalties lie. Upon what occasion did the Braves join Major League Baseball in retiring a #42 jersey in 1997?

THE ROOKIES

QUESTION 6: Alvin Dark became the first player in franchise history to win Rookie of the Year honors when he won the Major League award in 1948. Do you know which one of the following players did *not* win Rookie of the Year honors?
- a) Earl Williams
- b) Hank Aaron
- c) Samuel Jethroe

QUESTION 7: One Braves rookie set a record while playing on the biggest stage of all—the World Series. Do you know which one of the following players homered in his first two World Series at bats, and became the youngest rookie to ever hit a World Series home run?
- a) Andruw Jones
- b) Chipper Jones
- c) Rafael Furcal

QUESTION 8: Which Braves rookie saved 19 games, posted a 2.06 earned run average, and placed second in Rookie of the Year balloting in 1993? This same rookie, unfortunately, lost Game 1 of the League Championship Series vs. Philadelphia and then blew a crucial save opportunity during the ninth inning of Game 5—and the Phillies won in six games.
   a)   Mark Wohlers
   b)   Pedro Borbon
   c)   Greg McMichael

QUESTION 9: In 1995, the Braves boasted four players with 20-plus homers each for the first time since 1973: Fred McGriff, David Justice, Ryan Klesko, and . . . which Braves rookie?
   a)   Chipper Jones
   b)   Javy Lopez
   c)   Mike Kelly

QUESTION 10: Which Brave made the jump from Class A ball to the majors as a nineteen-year-old and went on to steal a franchise rookie record 40 bases . . . only to have reports surface later that proved he had actually been a *22-year-old* rookie?
   a)   Ron Gant
   b)   Rafael Furcal
   c)   Gerald Perry

THE VETERANS

QUESTION 11: Which of the following statements surrounding the Braves acquisition of veteran slugger Fred McGriff in July, 1993, is true?
   a)   There was a fire in the press box prior to his first game
   b)   McGriff hit a game-tying homer in the sixth inning of his first game
   c)   The Braves rallied from a 5-0 deficit to beat the Cardinals 8-5 in his first game
   d)   All of the above

QUESTION 12: Which veteran Braves player, who had the misfortune of being a career .299 hitter, became the first write-in candidate to start the All-Star Game for the National League in 1970?
- a) Rico Carty
- b) Orlando Cepeda
- c) Felix Milan
- d) Clete Boyer

QUESTION 13: Lonnie Smith was a seasoned veteran with a reputation for winning when he signed with the Braves in 1988. He'd already won three World Series titles and he became the first player in baseball history to play in the World Series with four different teams when Atlanta won the pennant in 1991. Smith won his first three trips to the World Series (1980, 1982, and 1985) but unfortunately he lost twice (1991 and 1992) with Atlanta. Can you identify the three teams that Smith won titles with?
- a) Royals, Brewers, Blue Jays
- b) Phillies, Cardinals, Royals
- c) Royals, Cardinals, Blue Jays
- d) Phillies, Brewers, Royals

QUESTION 14: In 2002, the Braves pitching staff led the league in ERA for the ninth time in a span of 12 seasons—and the bullpen was the best in the business. John Smoltz anchored the bullpen as the team's closer, but he got plenty of help. Can you identify the veteran reliever who was 7-2 with a 0.95 earned run average in 76 innings of work for the Braves in 2002, despite *not* pitching in the majors since *retiring* in 1998?
- a) Chris Hammond
- b) Darren Holmes
- c) Mike Remlinger
- d) Albie Lopez

QUESTION 15: In 2008, Atlanta's starting rotation included four veterans who were all former 20-game winners: Tim Hudson, Mike Hampton, Tom Glavine, and John Smoltz. The only problem was all four spent at least three months on the disabled list and three of them had season-ending surgery. Which starter was the only former 20-game winner in the Braves 2008 rotation who did *not* have season-ending surgery?
  a) Tim Hudson
  b) Mike Hampton
  c) Tom Glavine
  d) John Smoltz

THE LEGENDS

QUESTION 16: Which Hall of Famer is the only Brave in franchise history to play for the club in Boston, Milwaukee, and Atlanta (he was also the first—and so far only—player to play for one franchise in three different cities)?
  a) Eddie Mathews
  b) Warren Spahn
  c) Hank Aaron

QUESTION 17: Which Hall of Famer's three-year $600,000 contract with the Braves made him the first player in baseball history to earn $200,000 per year?
  a) Orlando Cepeda
  b) Phil Niekro
  c) Hank Aaron

QUESTION 18: Which Braves legend played a major league record 24 seasons without making a trip to the World Series?
  a) Gaylord Perry
  b) Bruce Sutter
  c) Phil Niekro

QUESTION 19: Curt Simmons, a former left-handed pitcher, once said of this Braves legend: "Trying to throw a fastball by [him] is like trying to sneak a sunrise past a rooster." Which Braves legend was he talking about?
   a) Orlando Cepeda
   b) Hank Aaron
   c) Eddie Mathews

QUESTION 20: The first athlete ever featured on the cover of *Sports Illustrated* was a Brave. Do you know which one?
   a) Babe Ruth
   b) Hank Aaron
   c) Eddie Mathews

THE HITTERS

QUESTION 21: Atlanta beat the Washington Nationals 10-4 on August 14, 2006, at RFK Stadium. The Braves hit four homers in that game, including three for this slugger—the first three-homer game of his career. Can you name this powerful switch-hitter?

QUESTION 22: Dale Murphy won his first MVP Award in 1982. The Braves slugger later became the first player in franchise history to win multiple league MVP Awards. How many times did Murphy take home league MVP honors?

QUESTION 23: The Hank Aaron Award was established by Major League Baseball in 1999 to honor the 25th anniversary of Aaron surpassing Babe Ruth's all-time home run record. It is given annually to the top hitter in each league. Can you name the Braves player who became the first in franchise history to win the Hank Aaron Award when he was recognized in 2005?

QUESTION 24: The Braves 2008 season was disappointing in many respects, but one of the few highlights was the first career batting title for a longtime Brave. Can you name him?

QUESTION 25: On July 31, 2007, Atlanta acquired this slugger in a deal with the Texas Rangers in exchange for five players, including catching prospect Jarrod Saltalamacchia. He responded by batting .317 with 17 homers and 56 RBI in only 54 games. Can you name this player?

THE PITCHERS

QUESTION 26: Jered Weaver made his big league debut on May 27, 2006, starting and pitching seven shutout innings in a 10-1 victory for the Angels vs. Baltimore. His brother Jeff was already part of the Angels rotation. In addition to debuting in such fine form, Jered and Jeff became the 18th pair of brothers in major league history to start on the mound for the same team, in the same season. Can you name the brother-duo that both started games on the mound for Atlanta in 1974?

QUESTION 27: Tom Glavine captured the Braves first and last Cy Young Awards of the 1990s—and in doing so he also captured the Braves last Cy Young of the 20th century. Can you name the Hall of Famer who won the first Cy Young Award in franchise history?

QUESTION 28: Tom Glavine was also obviously part of the Braves "Fab Four" starting rotation in 1993, when the club boasted four starters with 15-plus wins. Can you name the other three Braves starters who posted at least 15 wins in 1993?

QUESTION 29: After a decade as a dominating starter, John Smoltz recorded his first save for the Braves on August 17, 2001. The next season as the fulltime closer he led the league and set a franchise record for saves. How many saves did Smoltz record in 2002?

QUESTION 30: In the June draft in 1982, Atlanta selected a future Hall of Fame hurler in the fourth round. Unfortunately he did not sign with the club, opting for college instead. In 1985, the Montreal Expos selected that same pitcher out of USC in the second round of the draft—and nearly 20 years later, on May 18, 2004, he pitched a perfect game at Turner Field . . . for the Diamondbacks. You have to wonder how good the 1990s would have been if the Braves had signed this guy . . . can you name him?

THE MANAGERS AND COACHES

QUESTION 31: Who was the Braves manager for exactly one game, a 2-1 loss at Three Rivers Stadium in Pittsburgh, in May, 1977?

QUESTION 32: Which Braves skipper became the first National League manager to record 100-plus wins in five different seasons?

QUESTION 33: This Braves manager played 18 seasons and 2,209 big league games without once earning a trip to the postseason. His first taste of October baseball was in 1982, when he guided Atlanta to a division title. Can you name this manager?

QUESTION 34: A former league MVP, he began his eighth season as the Braves hitting coach in 2009—can you name him?

QUESTION 35: He played ten seasons for Atlanta before spending nine years coaching with the Braves minor league affiliates—and in 2009, he began his 11th season as the Braves first base coach. Can you name him?

THE FABULOUS FEATS

Hank Aaron owns more major league batting records than any player in baseball history. The Hammer also broke what many people believed to be an "untouchable" record when he surpassed Babe Ruth on the all-time home run list. You can instantly replay the scene of Hank Aaron's historic 715th career home run in your mind, but . . . exactly how much trivia surrounding this fabulous feat can you recall? All five questions in this section are about that historic moment.

QUESTION 36: What is the exact date that Hammerin' Hank launched his 715th career home run?

QUESTION 37: Which division rival did Aaron hit the record-breaking blast against?

QUESTION 38: It was a 1-0 fastball that Aaron launched over the left field wall. Who was the pitcher that gave up the record-breaking homer?

QUESTION 39: It was a two-run shot in the fourth inning, and it tied the game 3-3 after Atlanta's third baseman reached on an E6 to start the inning. Atlanta was third in the league with 120 homers that season—a total that included a team high 25 from that same third baseman. Can you name the Braves slugger who was on base when Aaron hit the record-breaking homer?

QUESTION 40: Ron Reed started and got the victory for the Braves that day, and Buzz Capra struck out six and tossed three scoreless innings for the save—but the pitcher who gets remembered most often is the one who caught Aaron's homer in the Braves bullpen and then delivered it to Aaron while he celebrated at home plate with his teammates. Can you name this reliever, who later became a highly respected pitching coach?

THE TEAMS

Atlanta won the 1995 World Series in six games over the Cleveland Indians. The Braves clinched the series with a 1-0 victory at home in Game 6. All five questions in this section are about that title-clenching game.

QUESTION 41: Cleveland used six pitchers in Game 6—one, Paul Assenmacher, began his career with the Braves, and three others later played for Atlanta: starter Dennis Martinez, and relievers Alan Embree and Julian Tavarez. Atlanta used only two pitchers. Who tossed eight shutout innings while giving up just one hit as the Braves Game 6 starter?
   a) Steve Avery
   b) Tom Glavine
   c) Greg Maddux
   d) John Smoltz

QUESTION 42: The only run of the game was a sixth-inning solo homer against lefty reliever Jim Poole. Who hit the game-winning blast for Atlanta?
   a) Chipper Jones
   b) Fred McGriff
   c) David Justice
   d) Ryan Klesko

QUESTION 43: Tony Pena got the Indians only hit of the game, a single in the sixth inning. Mark Wohlers pitched a perfect ninth to clinch the title for Atlanta. Who did Wohlers retire for the final out of the game?
   a) Albert Belle
   b) Manny Ramirez
   c) Jim Thome
   d) Carlos Baerga

QUESTION 44: Which Braves player caught the final out of the game?

a) Mark Lemke
b) Marquis Grissom
c) Javy Lopez
d) David Justice

QUESTION 45: Which Braves player earned series MVP honors?
a) Steve Avery
b) Tom Glavine
c) Greg Maddux
d) John Smoltz

MISCELLANEOUS

QUESTION 46: Chipper Jones is going to the Hall of Fame as a third baseman, but in 2002 he moved to left field in an effort to help improve the team, which had acquired a slugging third baseman from the Houston Astros. Chipper, of course, later moved back to third base, but can you name the Braves everyday third baseman in 2002?

QUESTION 47: Brian McCann earned his fourth trip to the All-Star Game in 2009, and yet he was only 25-years-old. The last time a Braves player made four trips to the All-Star Game by that age was 1966—and he was a catcher as well. Can you name him?

QUESTION 48: Just days prior to the 2009 All-Star break, the Braves front office made a surprising move when it traded popular outfielder Jeff Francoeur to the New York Mets, of all teams, for . . . what outfielder?

QUESTION 49: This relief pitcher once converted 28 consecutive save opportunities for the Pirates, and he saved a career high 24 games in 2006 before coming to Atlanta in a trade that sent Adam LaRoche to Pittsburgh. Can you name this lefty?

QUESTION 50: A former first-round draft pick, this sweet-swinging lefty began his career as an outfielder but was later converted to second base (it was Glenn Hubbard who spent countless hours in the offseason working with him on that transition). In 2008, he put together a 22-game hitting streak that included ten multi-hit games and 15 extra-base hits. Can you name him?

Chapter One Answer Key

Time to find out how you did—put a check mark next to the questions you answered correctly, and when you are done be sure and add up your score to find out your IQ, and to find out if you made the Opening Day roster.

THE NUMBERS GAME
- _ Question 1:   3
- _ Question 2:   21
- _ Question 3:   35
- _ Question 4:   41
- _ Question 5:   44

    Bonus: 31
    Bonus: 50th anniversary of Jackie Robinson's big league
               debut

THE ROOKIES
- _ Question 6:   B – Hank Aaron
- _ Question 7:   A – Andruw Jones, he was only 19, and he did it at Yankee Stadium, breaking the old record held by none other than Mickey Mantle
- _ Question 8:   C – Greg McMichael
- _ Question 9:   A – Chipper Jones
- _ Question 10:   B – Rafael Furcal

THE VETERANS
- _ Question 11:   D – All of the above
- _ Question 12:   A – Rico Carty
- _ Question 13:   B – Phillies, Cardinals, Royals
- _ Question 14:   A – Chris Hammond
- _ Question 15:   B – Mike Hampton

THE LEGENDS

_ Question 16:	A – Eddie Mathews
_ Question 17:	C – Hank Aaron
_ Question 18:	C – Phil Niekro
_ Question 19:	B – Hank Aaron
_ Question 20:	C – Eddie Mathews

THE HITTERS

_ Question 21:   Chipper Jones
_ Question 22:   2 – 1982 & 1983
_ Question 23:   Andruw Jones
_ Question 24:   Chipper Jones
_ Question 25:   Mark Teixeira

THE PITCHERS

_ Question 26:   Joe and Phil Niekro
_ Question 27:   Warren Spahn, 1957
_ Question 28:   Greg Maddux, John Smoltz, & Steve Avery
_ Question 29:   55
_ Question 30:   Randy Johnson

THE MANAGERS AND COACHES

_ Question 31:   Ted Turner
_ Question 32:   Bobby Cox
_ Question 33:   Joe Torre
_ Question 34:   Terry Pendleton
_ Question 35:   Glenn Hubbard

THE FABULOUS FEATS

_ Question 36:   April 8, 1974
_ Question 37:   Los Angeles Dodgers
_ Question 38:   Al Downing, he is remembered primarily for giving up Aaron's home run, but he should also be known for what he did in 1961, when he became the first African

                            American starting pitcher in New York Yankees history

__ Question 39:   Darrell Evans

__ Question 40:   Tom House

THE TEAMS

__ Question 41:   B – Tom Glavine

__ Question 42:   C – David Justice

__ Question 43:   D – Carlos Baerga

__ Question 44:   B – Marquis Grissom

__ Question 45:   B – Tom Glavine

MISCELLANEOUS

__ Question 46:   Vinny Castilla

__ Question 47:   Joe Torre

__ Question 48:   Ryan Church

__ Question 49:   Mike Gonzalez

__ Question 50:   Kelly Johnson

Got your Spring Training total? Here's how it breaks down:

NO DROP STATUS IN FANTASY LEAGUES EVERYWHERE	= 45-50
OPENING DAY STARTER	= 40-44
YOU MADE IT TO THE SHOW	= 35-39
PLATOON PLAYER AT BEST	= 30-34
ANOTHER SEASON IN THE MINORS	= 00-29

Good luck on Opening Day!

Chapter Two

OPENING DAY

THEY ALL COUNT NOW, no pressure. You made the roster with the big club and now you're looking forward to earning a big contract, some major endorsements perhaps, or being a part of the Sunday Conversation on SportsCenter, but most importantly, you're here to win the big game. So game on, let's find out how well you can do after we ratchet things up a notch. The categories stay the same, but everything else is more intense. We're about to find out whether or not you can play this game for a living.

THE NUMBERS GAME

QUESTION 51: Matt Diaz made his big league debut for Tampa in 2003, but it was with the Braves in 2006 that he got his first shot at significant playing time. Diaz responded by batting .327, and along the way he tied a N.L. record for hits in consecutive at bats. In how many consecutive at bats from August 12-14 did Diaz record a hit?

QUESTION 52: To follow-up on Diaz, in 2006 he also tied a franchise record first set by Rowland Office in 1975 for most consecutive pinch-hits. In how many consecutive at bats as a pinch-hitter did Diaz hit safely?

QUESTION 53: Warren Spahn won 356 games for the Braves—the most in franchise history. His *career* wins total is sixth highest in baseball history. How many *career* games did Warren Spahn win?

QUESTION 54: Braves fans remember 1992 for a lot of reasons, all of them related to clutch, dramatic performances, one after another, by Braves players. This is illustrated perfectly by this number—a franchise record set by the 1992 club—and the category is pinch-hit homers. How many times did Bobby Cox call on a pinch-hitter that season and get a long ball as the result?

QUESTION 55: Andruw Jones hit a franchise record 51 homers in 2005. Chipper Jones set a franchise record for switch-hitters when he blasted 45 homers in 1999. And in 1973 Darrell Evans set a franchise record for homers by a left-handed batter. How many homers did Evans hit to earn that distinction?

THE ROOKIES

QUESTION 56: The Braves won a lot of division titles under Bobby Cox on the strength of starting pitching. In 2006, Cox sent a rookie to the mound for his first career start on June 25 vs. Tampa, and all that rookie did was deliver eight innings of two-hit ball while surrendering one unearned run in a 4-1 victory. That same rookie tossed seven scoreless frames against Philly on September 14 to improve his record to 10-3. Only two other pitchers in baseball won as many games that season between June 25 and September 14: Jon Garland (11) and Johan Santana (10). Can you name the Braves lefty who began his career in such fine form?

QUESTION 57: The Braves pitching staff gave up only 649 earned runs in 2000—the lowest total in the league—and the club won 95 games and another division title. It wasn't all pitching, however, as Atlanta's offense also scored 810 runs—including 87 (third on the club) for this switch-hitter who claimed Rookie of the Year honors. Can you name this Braves superstar?

QUESTION 58: After getting a no-decision in his first major league start vs. Milwaukee on June 7, 2009, this Braves rookie reeled off four wins in a row, tossed 20 straight scoreless innings, and did not give up any runs in three consecutive starts—something no other Braves rookie had ever done during baseball's modern era. No wonder he was consistently rated as one of the Braves top prospects in the minors. Can you name this young gun?

QUESTION 59: As a follow-up, prior to 2009 the last time a Braves rookie pitcher tossed 20 consecutive scoreless innings was 1988. He tossed three shutouts in 1988, but despite pitching 11 seasons in the majors his career shutout total was only . . . four. Can you name the Braves rookie who tossed 20 consecutive shutout innings in 1988?

QUESTION 60: And one more follow-up question, in baseball's modern era only one other Braves rookie posted a 4-0 record after five career games with the big club. Atlanta's first pick and the overall #6 selection in the 1974 amateur draft, this tall lefty was 9-3 with a 2.81 earned run average as a rookie in 1978—and he was 4-0 after his first five games. Can you name him?

THE VETERANS

QUESTION 61: After the trade deadline every MLB team places players on waivers. Any player that clears waivers can be traded after the deadline, but if he is claimed off waivers then he must either be recalled from the list or traded to the team that claimed him. In August, 2006, Andruw Jones did not clear waivers, forcing the Braves to either trade or recall the All-Star outfielder. Jones had played his entire career for Atlanta—more than 1,500 games. In the 25 seasons prior to 2006 there was only one instance in which a player was traded midseason after spending every one of at least 1,500 career games for his original team—and that player was traded by the Braves. Atlanta recalled Jones in 2006. Can you name the veteran who *was* traded by the Braves after spending the first 1,926 games of his career with the club?

QUESTION 62: The Roberto Clemente Award is given annually by Major League Baseball to a player "who demonstrates the values Clemente displayed in his commitment to community and understanding the value of helping others" (MLB.com). Can you name the Braves veteran pitcher—and future Hall of Famer—who in 2005 became the first player in franchise history to win the Roberto Clemente Award?

QUESTION 63: The Braves not only won the N.L. West in 1991, but the club also won numerous prestigious individual and team honors. Bobby Cox won Manager of the Year, John Schuerholz won Executive of the Year, and Atlanta was named Organization of the Year by *Baseball America*—not to mention on the field, where this veteran third baseman won both the league batting title and league MVP honors . . . can you name him?

QUESTION 64: The Braves had two Silver Slugger recipients in 1997, and it was the first such award for both players. One was pitcher John Smoltz—and the other was a .262 career hitter. Can you name the other Braves veteran who won his only career Silver Slugger that season, and who also became the first shortstop in franchise history to win the award?

QUESTION 65: According to the Elias Sports Bureau, only four pitchers who began their career in 1950 or later have won 244 or more games for the same team. Jim Palmer (268, Baltimore) and Bob Gibson (251, St. Louis) are two of them—and the other two both pitched for the Braves. One is already in the Hall of Fame and the other is a future Hall of Famer—can you name them?

THE LEGENDS

QUESTION 66: Hank Aaron is baseball's all-time RBI leader with 2,297. His career high 132 RBI came in 1957, but that number represents only the second highest total for a Braves player during the 20th century. Can you identify the legend that drove home 135 runs for the Braves highest season effort in the 20th century?

- a) Dale Murphy
- b) Eddie Mathews
- c) Chipper Jones
- d) Wally Berger

QUESTION 67: Hank Aaron hit at least one homer in 31 different stadiums. He hit 534 homers vs. right-handed pitchers and 221 homers vs. left-handed pitchers. He hit 385 at home, and 370 on the road. All those home runs, there had to be one pitcher he punished more than any other—and as it happens, the guy he took yard more often than anyone else is in the Hall of Fame. Which pitcher gave up more home runs (17) to Hank Aaron than any other pitcher in history?

- a) Robin Roberts
- b) Juan Marichal
- c) Don Drysdale
- d) Sandy Koufax

QUESTION 68: So we've established there was no shame in giving up the long ball to Bad Henry. Can you identify the Hall of Fame legend that was on the mound to serve up Aaron's 600th career home run?

- a) Gaylord Perry
- b) Steve Carlton
- c) Nolan Ryan
- d) Tom Seaver

QUESTION 69: Babe Ruth hit a home run in his first at bat wearing a Braves uniform in 1935, his final big league season.

Can you identify the pitching legend who gave up that long ball?
   a) Dizzy Dean
   b) Carl Hubbell
   c) Dutch Leonard
   d) Larry French

QUESTION 70: Ty Cobb once said, "I've known three or four perfect swings in my time—this boy's got one of them." What Braves legend was Cobb referring to when he made that statement?
   a) Hank Aaron
   b) Joe Adcock
   c) Eddie Mathews
   d) Johnny Logan

THE HITTERS

QUESTION 71: Javy Lopez hit 260 career homers, including 214 with the Braves. Lopez also set a major league record in 2003 for most home runs by a catcher in a single season. How many bombs did Lopez launch that season *as a catcher*?
   a) 41
   b) 42
   c) 43
   d) 44

QUESTION 72: Who won more Silver Slugger Awards for Atlanta from 1995-2008.
   a) Tom Glavine
   b) John Smoltz
   c) Chipper Jones
   d) Andruw Jones

QUESTION 73: The Braves have been home to more than a few big name sluggers, and some of those sluggers have won MVP honors. What was the season home run total for the first league MVP recipient in franchise history? See if you can identify the correct range from the following:

a) 9 or fewer
b) 10-19
c) 20-29
d) 30 or more

QUESTION 74: Atlanta won its second consecutive pennant in 1992 but lost in six games to the Toronto Blue Jays in the World Series. The Braves batted just .220 as a team in the series. Ron Gant batted only .125, David Justice batted only .158, and Terry Pendleton batted only .240. Atlanta did have one offensive star in the series—a speedster, he batted .533 (8 for 15) with four runs, two doubles, two walks, and five steals . . . do you know who these numbers belong to?

a) Deion Sanders
b) Otis Nixon
c) Lonnie Smith
d) Brian Hunter

QUESTION 75: Hall of Famer Eddie Mathews ranks among the top 25 home run hitters in baseball history. Do you know how many 30-plus homer seasons Mathews had with the Braves?

a) 7
b) 8
c) 9
d) 10

BONUS QUESTION: To follow-up on Eddie Mathews, the slugger launched 40-plus homers in a season four times, but do you know how many times he led the league in homers?

THE PITCHERS

QUESTION 76: Derek Lowe, who got the ball against Philly to start 2009, was only the third Braves pitcher since 1921 to make his debut for the club by starting on Opening Day. Gary Gentry got the nod in 1973. Can you identify the third hurler to debut in that fashion?
  a) Greg Maddux
  b) John Smoltz
  c) Tim Hudson

QUESTION 77: Leo Mazzone became a household name for the way he handled the Braves pitching staff. You might say he won a few Cy Young Awards himself in the 1990s. As it is, Greg Maddux, Tom Glavine, and John Smoltz all took home at least one Cy Young apiece. How many Cy Young Awards did the Braves Big Three combine to win during the 1990s (not including the award Maddux won with the Cubs)?
  a) 5
  b) 6
  c) 7

QUESTION 78: Phil Niekro made a franchise record nine career starts on Opening Day. Do you know which of Atlanta's Big Three from the Bobby Cox managerial era got the nod the most times on Opening Day?
  a) John Smoltz
  b) Tom Glavine
  c) Greg Maddux

QUESTION 79: To follow-up on Phil Niekro, after beginning his career pitching out of the bullpen the Hall of Famer won 15-plus games in a season 12 times—including 1985, when the 46-year-old hurler won 16 games for the Yankees despite being the oldest player in baseball for the second consecutive season. How many times did Niekro win 20-plus games while pitching for the Braves?

- a)   1
- b)   3
- c)   5

QUESTION 80: Warren Spahn won 20-plus games 13 times—a National League record. How many times did the Hall of Famer lead the league in wins?

- a)   4
- b)   6
- c)   8

THE MANAGERS AND COACHES

QUESTION 81: Numerous Hall of Famers called the shots from the Braves dugout at one time or another, but only one can claim to be the first skipper in franchise history. Can you identify him?

- a)   Harry Wright
- b)   Frank Selee
- c)   King Kelly
- d)   Joe Kelley

QUESTION 82: Bobby Cox and Hall of Fame manager Frank Selee are the only skippers in franchise history to lead the Braves for more than a decade—and Cox has done it for more than two decades. Joe Torre replaced Cox in the Braves dugout in 1982, but after Torre the Braves went through an additional four skippers before Cox returned to the dugout in mid-1990. Who was the last man at the Braves helm prior to Cox returning as manager after 65 games in the 1990 season?

- a)   Chuck Tanner
- b)   Russ Nixon
- c)   Eddie Haas
- d)   Bobby Wine

QUESTION 83: Which Hall of Fame manager never placed higher than fifth during six seasons with the Braves franchise, but later won ten pennants managing in the American League?
  a) Frank Selee
  b) Bill McKechnie
  c) Dave Bancroft
  d) Casey Stengel

QUESTION 84: Who was the Braves manager that led the club to victory in the 1914 World Series?
  a) Johnny Kling
  b) Fred Tenney
  c) George Stallings
  d) Fred Mitchell

QUESTION 85: After guiding the Braves to a division title in 1969, the first year of division play, this manager won only 76 games in 1970, 82 games in 1971, and was struggling with a 47-57 record when he was fired in 1972. Can you identify the skipper who won the Braves first division title in 1969?
  a) Bobby Bragan
  b) Billy Hitchcock
  c) Ken Silvestri
  d) Luman Harris

THE FABULOUS FEATS

QUESTION 86: Hank Aaron was the first player in baseball history to amass 500 homers and 3,000 hits. He reached the 500-homer plateau first. Do you know what year it was when Aaron recorded his 3,000th career hit?
  a) 1968
  b) 1970
  c) 1972

QUESTION 87: Staying with the Hammer here—can you identify the fabulous feat he accomplished in 1963?
   a) 30/30 club
   b) 30-game hitting streak
   c) Tenth consecutive 30-homer season

QUESTION 88: After surprising the baseball world by winning the N.L. West in 1991, the Braves defeated the Pittsburgh Pirates in a thrilling seven-game series to claim the pennant as well. Atlanta won Games 2 and 6 by the same score: 1-0. In both instances the Pirates had won the previous game, and in both instances the same Braves pitcher responded with eight-plus shutout innings. Can you name the Braves lefty who won series MVP honors after posting a 2-0 record? His line for the series: 16.1 IP, 9 H, 4 BB, 17 K, 0 R.
   a) Tom Glavine
   b) Steve Avery
   c) Charlie Leibrandt

QUESTION 89: Atlanta set a franchise record on May 1, 1985, in a 17-9 victory vs. Cincinnati. Rick Mahler got the win to improve his record to 6-0, despite giving up five runs in five innings of work. Mahler, however, did contribute to the team record set that day, as he was 2 for 4 at the plate. The offense was clicking so well that reliever Gene Garber got a hit and combined with Mahler to go 3 for 5 with two runs and an RBI. Dale Murphy hit the Braves only homer of the game, just one of his three hits (he also scored four runs and drove in three). All total the offense tallied the most hits in a single game in franchise history. How many hits did the Braves get that day?
   a) 25
   b) 27
   c) 29

QUESTION 90: On July 27, 2009, A.J. Burnett and two relievers combined to pitch a one-hit shutout for the New York Yankees vs. the New York Mets—this, after CC Sabathia and the bullpen held the Mets to only three hits the previous night. It was the first time since 1965 that the Mets lineup was held to as few as four hits total for back-to-back games. The Braves beat the Mets 3-1 and 9-0 in consecutive games on September 10-11, 1965. How many hits did the Braves limit the Mets to during those two games?

  a) 2
  b) 3
  c) 4

THE TEAMS

QUESTION 91: Atlanta lost the 1992 World Series to the Toronto Blue Jays in six games. After taking the series opener 3-1 at home, the Braves lost Games 2, 3, and 4. Atlanta won Game 5 to stay alive, but lost the series at home when Toronto took Game 6 in extra-innings. Atlanta won only two games in the series, but in terms of total runs the Braves offense outscored the Blue Jays. How many one-run games did the Braves lose in the 1992 World Series?

  a) 1
  b) 2
  c) 3
  d) 4

QUESTION 92: Division play began in 1969, and the Braves joined San Francisco, Cincinnati, Los Angeles, Houston, and San Diego to form the original N.L. West. Atlanta was led by Phil Niekro on the mound and Hank Aaron at the plate, and with a record of 93-69 the Braves claimed the first division title in franchise history. The Giants were in first place on September 6, however, when the Braves trailed by their largest margin of the season. In what place in the division standings were the Braves after play

concluded on September 6?
   a) Third
   b) Fourth
   c) Fifth
   d) Last

QUESTION 93: Atlanta became the first team in league history to go from worst-to-first when it won the N.L. West in 1991. It was not easy, however, as the Braves trailed the Dodgers by 9.5 games at the break. It took a season high eight-game winning streak in the final week-and-a-half of the schedule to clinch the title on October 5. How many games did Atlanta win on the road during that title-clenching eight-game streak in September and October?
   a) 0
   b) 2
   c) 4
   d) 6

QUESTION 94: Atlanta trailed the Dodgers by two games when it won the first of eight straight on September 27, 1991. The Braves won four straight and moved to within a single game of LA, but that was in jeopardy when Braves starter Charlie Leibrandt gave up six runs in the first inning against Cincinnati on October 1. The Braves rallied, however, and won in heroic fashion with a two-run homer in the ninth inning against the defending world champions ace closer Rob Dibble. Who was the slugger that gave the Braves an improbable 7-6 win to keep the club's hopes alive?
   a) Ron Gant
   b) David Justice
   c) Sid Bream
   d) Terry Pendleton

QUESTION 95: Atlanta won its second consecutive pennant in 1992, but again it took a long winning streak to get the job done. The Braves were in last place on May 27, trailing the Giants by seven games with a 20-27 record. Atlanta won 21 of 24 afterwards, posted an incredible 78-37 record the rest of the way, and tied a franchise record winning streak in July to move into first place. How many consecutive games did the Braves win in July, 1992?

    a) 11
    b) 13
    c) 15
    d) 17

MISCELLANEOUS

QUESTION 96: It's easy for Braves fans to consider 1995 to be a year of destiny, after all, the club won a major league best 31 games by a single run and a N.L. best 25 games in their final at bat. Not only that, but an overwhelming majority of the Braves "last at bat" wins came *after* July 3. How many times after July 3 did Atlanta win in its final at bat?

    a) 14
    b) 16
    c) 18
    d) 20

QUESTION 97: The Braves began play in Atlanta on April 12, 1966, by losing a tough game, 3-2 in 13 innings. Which team spoiled the Braves debut in Atlanta?

    a) Dodgers
    b) Giants
    c) Pirates
    d) Phillies

QUESTION 98: Atlanta signed Japanese star Kenshin Kawakami as a free agent prior to the 2009 season. Kawakami was a former Rookie of the Year and Most Valuable Player in Japan's Central League, and in 2007 he also won a championship as his team claimed the Japan Series. Do you know which team Kawakami pitched for in Japan?

a) Chunichi Dragons
b) Hanshin Tigers
c) Yomiuri Giants
d) Tokyo Yakult Swallows

QUESTION 99: Atlanta selected Chipper Jones #1 overall in the 1990 amateur draft. It was a good year for Chipper, to understate things just a bit, seeing as he was named the Florida High School Player of the Year and he also led his team to a state championship. After Chipper became a star for the Braves he went back and built a heck-of-a nice locker room for his high school's baseball program. What prestigious prep school in Jacksonville, Florida, did Chipper graduate from?

a) San Jose Episcopal Day School
b) The Bolles School
c) University Christian School
d) Bishop Kenny High School

QUESTION 100: Which player owns two of the top five season totals in franchise history for doubles (through 2008)?

a) Marcus Giles
b) Wally Berger
c) Gerald Perry
d) Chipper Jones

Chapter Two Answer Key

Time to find out how you did—put a check mark next to the questions you answered correctly, and when you are done be sure and add up your score to find out your IQ, and to find out if you deserve a shot at the Mid-Summer Classic.

THE NUMBERS GAME

_ Question 51:	10
_ Question 52:	5
_ Question 53:	363
_ Question 54:	9
_ Question 55:	41

THE ROOKIES

_ Question 56:	Chuck James
_ Question 57:	Rafael Furcal
_ Question 58:	Tommy Hanson
_ Question 59:	Pete Smith
_ Question 60:	Larry McWilliams

THE VETERANS

_ Question 61:	Dale Murphy to Philly, 1990
_ Question 62:	John Smoltz
_ Question 63:	Terry Pendleton
_ Question 64:	Jeff Blauser
_ Question 65:	Phil Niekro, 268, & Tom Glavine, 244

THE LEGENDS

_ Question 66:	B – Eddie Mathews, 1953
_ Question 67:	C – Don Drysdale
_ Question 68:	A – Gaylord Perry, but Carlton (#610), Ryan (#606), and Seaver (#615) weren't far off
_ Question 69:	B – Carl Hubbell

__ Question 70:   C – Eddie Mathews

THE HITTERS
__ Question 71:   B – he hit 43 total, but only 42 as a catcher
__ Question 72:   A – Tom Glavine
__ Question 73:   A – Johnny Evers won MVP honors in
                     1914 despite hitting only one home run
__ Question 74:   A – Deion Sanders
__ Question 75:   D – 10

Bonus Question: 2, with 47 in 1953 and 46 in 1956

THE PITCHERS
__ Question 76:   A – Greg Maddux
__ Question 77:   B – 6
__ Question 78:   C – Maddux 7, Glavine & Smoltz 4 each
__ Question 79:   B – 3, two of which led the league: 1974
                     and 1979
__ Question 80:   C – 8, which is a major league record

THE MANAGERS AND COACHES
__ Question 81:   A – Harry Wright
__ Question 82:   B – Russ Nixon
__ Question 83:   D – Casey Stengel
__ Question 84:   C – George Stallings
__ Question 85:   D – Luman Harris

THE FABULOUS FEATS
__ Question 86:   B – May 17, 1970
__ Question 87:   A – 31 steals, 44 homers
__ Question 88:   B – Steve Avery
__ Question 89:   A – 25
__ Question 90:   A – 2

THE TEAMS

- __ Question 91:   D – 4
- __ Question 92:   B – fourth place, three games out of first behind the Giants, Reds, and Dodgers
- __ Question 93:   D – 6, 3 at Houston, 3 at Cincinnati
- __ Question 94:   B – David Justice
- __ Question 95:   B – 13, July 8-25, and the Braves took over first place on July 22

MISCELLANEOUS

- __ Question 96:   C – 18
- __ Question 97:   C – Pirates
- __ Question 98:   A – Chunichi Dragons
- __ Question 99:   B – The Bolles School
- __ Question 100:   A – Marcus Giles

Got your Opening Day total? Here's how it breaks down:

MLB PLAYER OF THE MONTH FOR APRIL	= 45-50
SCOTT BORAS WANTS TO REPRESENT YOU	= 40-44
YOU'RE STILL IN THE SHOW	= 35-39
STRUGGLING TO GET PLAYING TIME	= 30-34
YOU JUST GOT SENT DOWN	= 00-29

Good luck in the All-Star balloting!

Chapter Three

ALL-STAR

So you want to be an All-Star, no problem. All you have to do is to bring your "A" game to the park every day, your absolute best, day in, day out, because only a select few make it to that upper echelon where you hear things like "franchise player" or "future Hall of Famer." Oh, and one more thing . . . you have to be better than almost everyone else to make it, which means for some of you, well, your "A" game might not be enough. You better work hard. I mean, really hard. You do well here and you will not only have shown us something special, but you will also have earned yourself some well-deserved recognition. Let's get to it.

THE NUMBERS GAME

QUESTION 101: Dale Murphy hit 36 home runs in three consecutive seasons from 1982-84. In total, Murphy had six 30-plus homer seasons. How many home run titles did he win?

    a)   0
    b)   1
    c)   2
    d)   3

QUESTION 102: Dale Murphy hit a career high 44 homers in 1987. Chipper Jones hit a career high 45 homers in 1999. Hank Aaron hit a career high 47 homers in 1971, and Andruw Jones set his career high with 51 homers in 2005. How many home run titles were won during those four career high efforts?

    a) 0
    b) 1
    c) 2
    d) 3

QUESTION 103: Hank Aaron hit at least one home run against 310 different pitchers, including 12 who made it to the Hall of Fame. He hit 124 first inning homers, 400 solo homers, and he even hit three pinch-hit homers. During a career in which he went yard 755 times, Aaron also had 62 multi-home run games. How many times did Aaron hit *three bombs* in one game?

    a) 0
    b) 1
    c) 2
    d) 3

QUESTION 104: Every team goes through cycles—for pitching, offense, defense, and winning in general—and some years are just better than others for seemingly no other reason. Atlanta set a franchise record for futility in 1968, but it set a franchise record for productivity in 2003—the 1968 club scored the fewest runs in the Atlanta era of team history, while the 2003 club scored the most. Can you pick out the correct runs totals for those two seasons?

    a) 514 and 907
    b) 589 and 936
    c) 603 and 947
    d) 609 and 988

QUESTION 105: There is something special about batting with the bases juiced, and every batter who steps into the box with the bags full thinks at least momentarily about going yard and bringing them all home. The Braves set a franchise record in 1997 for doing just that—do you know how many grand slams

the club hit that season?
- a) 8
- b) 10
- c) 12
- d) 14

BONUS QUESTION: To follow-up on the grand slams, in addition to the team franchise record, one Braves player set an individual franchise record by slugging three grand slams in 1997. Can you name this player?

THE ROOKIES

QUESTION 106: There have been many great performances by Braves rookies throughout the years. Can you identify the Braves slugger who became the first rookie in baseball history to launch three homers in a single game?
- a) Eddie Mathews
- b) Hank Aaron
- c) Bob Horner
- d) Ron Gant

QUESTION 107: Can you identify the slugger who set a record for most homers in a season by a rookie during the Atlanta era of team history?
- a) Eddie Mathews
- b) Chipper Jones
- c) Earl Williams
- d) Andruw Jones

QUESTION 108: Jair Jurrjens came to the Braves in the trade that sent Edgar Renteria to the Detroit Tigers. Jurrjens was third in Rookie of the Year balloting in 2008. Despite being only 22-years-old, in which of the following was Jurrjens the team leader

during his rookie season?
- a) 13 wins
- b) 188 innings
- c) 139 strikeouts
- d) All of the above

QUESTION 109: Which of the following hit the most homers during his rookie season with the Braves?
- a) Wally Berger
- b) Hank Aaron
- c) Eddie Mathews
- d) David Justice

QUESTION 110: Here are the rookie year won-loss totals for these four pitchers: 12-6, 3-11, 7-15, and 7-17. Which of the following managed to post the 12-6 record on the mound during his rookie season with Atlanta?
- a) Steve Avery
- b) Tom Glavine
- c) Pete Smith
- d) Damian Moss

THE VETERANS

QUESTION 111: Atlanta was unable to repeat as division champs in 1970, winning only 76 games all season, but there were some bright spots for the club—including a batting title for one of its veteran players. Can you identify the longtime Brave who batted .366 to win the 1970 league batting title?
- a) Hank Aaron
- b) Orlando Cepeda
- c) Felix Milan
- d) Rico Carty

QUESTION 112: Terry Pendleton spent 15 seasons in the big leagues, including some of his most productive as a veteran third baseman wearing a Braves uniform. He was instrumental in getting six of his teams to the postseason, and of those, five won the pennant and advanced to the World Series: 1985 Cardinals, 1987 Cardinals, 1991 Braves, 1992 Braves, and 1996 Braves. How many World Series titles did Pendleton win as a player?

    a) 0
    b) 1
    c) 2
    d) 3

QUESTION 113: Deacon White, Dan Brouthers, and Hugh Duffy all won batting titles for the Braves franchise prior to the turn of the 20th century—but which veteran player won the first batting title for the Braves franchise during baseball's modern era?

    a) Ernie Lombardi
    b) Rogers Hornsby
    c) Hank Aaron
    d) Rico Carty

QUESTION 114: This veteran hit a few memorable long balls in his career, including one on May 26, 1959, that broke up a no-hit bid by Harvey Haddix. The Pirates starter was perfect through 12, and still had a no-hitter with two men aboard in the 13th when he gave up the long ball. The Braves batter was called out, however, despite driving in the winning run, because as he was rounding the bases he passed one of the other base runners. So he hit the game-winning shot out of the park . . . but didn't get credit for a home run—now, which Braves veteran gets credit for that feat?

    a) Hank Aaron
    b) Eddie Mathews
    c) Joe Adcock
    d) Felix Mantilla

QUESTION 115: On June 8, 1961, the Braves became the first team in baseball history to hit four consecutive home runs. The Braves hit six homers total, including one by pitcher Warren Spahn who, despite the offensive outburst, lost to Cincinnati by a score of 10-8. A 20-year-old rookie named Joe Torre had a chance to make it five consecutive homers, but he grounded out to third. Do you know which four Braves became the first teammates in history to hit four consecutive home runs?

    a) Warren Spahn, Lee Maye, Frank Bolling, and Eddie Mathews

    b) Frank Bolling, Eddie Mathews, Hank Aaron, and Joe Adcock

    c) Charlie Lau, Warren Spahn, Lee Maye, and Frank Bolling

    d) Eddie Mathews, Hank Aaron, Joe Adcock, and Frank Thomas

THE LEGENDS

QUESTION 116: Eddie Mathews hit 493 of his 512 career home runs for the Braves. The Hall of Famer was traded by Atlanta after the 1966 season, despite being only seven homers shy of joining the 500-club. What team was Mathews playing for when he hit his 500th home run?

    a) Detroit Tigers

    b) Houston Astros

    c) St. Louis Cardinals

QUESTION 117: The first African-American player in franchise history made his debut in 1950. Can you correctly identify this Braves legend?

    a) Sam Jethroe

    b) Jim Pendleton

    c) Mack Jones

QUESTION 118: Which Braves legend holds the major league record with 121 career victories after the age of 40?
- a) Warren Spahn
- b) Phil Niekro
- c) Hoyt Wilhelm

QUESTION 119: Which Braves legend won 300-plus career games despite winning only 67 games prior to his 29th birthday?
- a) Tom Glavine
- b) Phil Niekro
- c) Warren Spahn

QUESTION 120: All three of the following pairs of sluggers homered during the same game on at least 56 different occasions, making them among the most prolific and feared dual threats in baseball history. Which of the pairs of Braves teammates holds the major league record with 75 times hitting a home run in the same game?
- a) Andruw Jones and Chipper Jones
- b) Eddie Mathews and Joe Adcock
- c) Hank Aaron and Eddie Mathews

THE HITTERS

QUESTION 121: Del Bissonette hit 25 of his 66 career home runs as a rookie in 1928. The Dodgers lefty first baseman hit ten of his 25 bombs against left-handed hurlers, setting a league record. The next time a rookie hit ten lefty vs. lefty homers in the N.L. was 1990. Can you name the Braves slugger who hit 28 homers as a rookie in 1990, including ten lefty vs. lefty bombs?

QUESTION 122: Gary Sheffield was second on the club with 39 homers in 2003. He hit his 35th home run vs. Pittsburgh on September 6, and with that blast he joined a select group of sluggers who all posted at least one 35-homer season with *three* *different* ball clubs. The list includes Reggie Jackson, Dave Kingman, and Albert Belle—and since Sheffield, Alex Rodriguez, Alfonso Soriano, and Jim Thome have added their names as well. Sheffield did one better. He hit 36 homers in 2004 for a *fourth* different team. Can you name the other three teams for which Gary Sheffield had at least one 35-homer season?

QUESTION 123: Chipper Jones and Andruw Jones combined to hit 641 home runs as teammates from 1997-2006. That number was easily the highest of any pair of teammates during that ten-year stretch, far outpacing the 528 hit by Astros sluggers Jeff Bagwell and Lance Berkman. The Joneses, however, still came up 51 big flies short of both the league and franchise record 692 combined homers hit by a pair of Braves sluggers during a ten-year stretch from 1954-63. Can you name the powerful duo that holds the record?

QUESTION 124: Braves pitchers combined to win four consecutive Silver Slugger Awards from 1995-98, but can you name the Braves slugger who became the first player in franchise history to win four consecutive Silver Slugger Awards?

QUESTION 125: In a span of six seasons from 2003-08, Braves catchers won four Silver Slugger Awards. How many different catchers won the award for Atlanta during that span—and can you name them all?

THE PITCHERS

QUESTION 126: John Smoltz started and pitched seven-plus shutout innings vs. Minnesota in Game 7 of the 1991 World Series, but the Braves lost a heartbreaker, 1-0 in ten innings. The Twins starter that day pitched a complete game. Atlanta won the pennant again in 1992. Tom Glavine started and pitched a complete game four-hitter vs. Toronto in Game 1 of the 1992 World Series . . . and the losing pitcher that day for the Blue Jays?

It was the same guy that beat the Braves for the Twins in Game 7 the year before. Can you name this pitcher?

QUESTION 127: Tom Glavine was the Braves Opening Day starter for the first time in 1990. Glavine was an integral part of the Braves staff that dominated that entire decade, and in fact, along with John Smoltz and Greg Maddux, one of Atlanta's Big Three got the nod on every Opening Day in the 1990s. It wasn't until 2001 that someone other than Glavine, Smoltz, or Maddux took the hill for the season's first game. Can you name the Braves 2001 Opening Day starter?

QUESTION 128: John Smoltz won 15 games for the first time in 1992, and he also led the league with 215 strikeouts. It was the first time a Braves hurler led the league in strikeouts in 15 years. Can you name the last player to lead the league in Ks for Atlanta prior to Smoltz in 1992?

QUESTION 129: Hall of Fame pitcher Ferguson Jenkins notched six consecutive 20-win seasons for the Cubs from 1967-72. It took more than 20 years before another N.L. hurler hit the 20-win plateau in as many as three consecutive seasons . . . and the guy who did it was wearing a Braves jersey. Can you name this future Hall of Famer?

QUESTION 130: Atlanta defeated the New York Yankees in seven games to win the 1957 World Series. Can you name the Braves pitcher who was 3-0 with a 0.67 earned run average in the series, beating Bobby Shantz 4-2 in Game 2, Whitey Ford 1-0 in Game 5, and Don Larsen 5-0 in Game 7?

THE MANAGERS AND COACHES

QUESTION 131: Longtime skipper Bobby Cox has been tossed by umpires a few times. Okay, a *record* number of times. On October 26, 1996, Cox was ejected from Game 6 of the World Series vs.

the Yankees after arguing with second base umpire Terry Tata when Marquis Grissom was gunned down by Joe Girardi on a controversial call in the fifth inning. It was a game-changing play because Chipper Jones led off the sixth with a double. As it turned out, the Braves did not score in the fifth or sixth, lost the game 3-2, and lost the series four games to two. Who was the umpire that tossed Bobby Cox that day?

  a) Gerry Davis
  b) Jim Evans
  c) Terry Tata
  d) Tim Welke

QUESTION 132: And speaking of Cox's ejection record . . . 132 was the magic number, when he topped the list for all-time ejections. He argued a called third strike on Chipper Jones and was tossed by plate umpire Ted Barrett. Afterwards, Cox said of the record, "It means nothing. It just means I've been around for a long time, that's all." He was much more concerned with the way the game ended. Chipper Jones hit a walk-off double to lift the Braves to a 5-4 victory vs. the Giants. As for the list Cox now finds himself at the top of, which of the following managers did he overtake with his 132nd career ejection?

  a) Tony LaRussa
  b) John McGraw
  c) Leo Durocher
  d) Earl Weaver

QUESTION 133: Bobby Cox's first tour of duty with Atlanta was from 1978-81. How many winning records did Cox and the Braves post during that time?

  a) 0
  b) 1
  c) 2
  d) 3

QUESTION 134: Which of the following statements about current (2009) Braves bullpen coach Eddie Perez are true?
- a) Spent 18 of 20 professional seasons as a player in the Braves organization
- b) Won MVP honors for Atlanta in the 1999 NLCS vs. the Mets
- c) Retired with the highest batting average (.464) in NLCS history for a catcher
- d) All of the above

QUESTION 135: Which current (2009) member of the Braves coaching staff won a World Series title during his playing days as a member of the Oakland Athletics?
- a) Roger McDowell
- b) Brian Snitker
- c) Glenn Hubbard
- d) Chino Cadahia

THE FABULOUS FEATS

QUESTION 136: The Braves tossed two no-hitters in 1960. It was the first (and so far only) time in franchise history that two pitchers threw a no-no for the Braves in the same season. Can you identify the duo that performed this phenomenal feat?
- a) Bob Buhl and Carl Willey
- b) Lew Burdette and Bob Buhl
- c) Warren Spahn and Lew Burdette
- d) Juan Pizarro and Warren Spahn

QUESTION 137: Joe Adcock was a powerful first baseman who played for the Braves in the 1950s. Adcock, who was on the club that beat the Yankees in the 1957 World Series, put on a tremendous offensive display vs. Brooklyn on July 31, 1954.

What remarkable feat did he accomplish that day?
    a) Hit for the cycle
    b) Hit two grand slams
    c) Hit safely in six consecutive at bats
    d) Hit four home runs

QUESTION 138: Brian McCann became the seventh player in franchise history to hit at least one home run in five consecutive team games when he went on a binge in 2006, from July 15-19. Can you identify the first player in franchise history to homer in five consecutive team games?
    a) Hank Aaron
    b) Jeff Burroughs
    c) Eddie Miller
    d) Rogers Hornsby

QUESTION 139: To follow-up on McCann, he was the first catcher in all of baseball to homer in five consecutive team games since Sandy Alomar did it for the Indians in 1997. McCann was also just the second catcher to ever homer in five consecutive games for the Braves. Can you identify the first catcher to do so?
    a) Dale Murphy
    b) Ozzie Virgil
    c) Ernie Whitt
    d) Jody Davis

QUESTION 140: You might recall that Pete Rose hit safely in 44 consecutive games in 1978, and you probably recall as well that it was the Braves pitching staff that brought that streak to an end. But on the subject of hitting streaks, do you have any idea who the first Braves player was to hit safely in 30 consecutive games during the Atlanta era of franchise history?
    a) Hank Aaron
    b) Alvin Dark
    c) Rico Carty
    d) Joe Torre

THE TEAMS

QUESTION 141: It is a sure sign of success when both Cy Young and Most Valuable Player honors are given to players on the same team. The Braves earned that distinction twice in the 20th century. Can you identify the correct pairs of seasons in which Braves players took top honors in both Cy Young and MVP balloting?
- a) 1991 and 1999
- b) 1983 and 1995
- c) 1957 and 1991
- d) 1957 and 1999

QUESTION 142: The phrase "Spahn and Sain and two days of rain"—or sometimes, "Spahn and Sain then pray for rain"— became a popular expression because of the phenomenal success of Braves hurlers Warren Spahn and Johnny Sain for what pennant-winning Braves team?
- a) 1948
- b) 1953
- c) 1957
- d) 1958

QUESTION 143: The 1993 Atlanta squad will forever be remembered because of its heart-pounding division race against the Giants, claimed by the Braves on the season's final day. It was the first time in division play history that any team won three straight N.L. West crowns, and once again the Braves had to overcome a large deficit. It took a 51-17 record in the season's second half to catch San Francisco (the third best second half surge in baseball history). How many games behind the Giants were the Braves as late as July 22?
- a) 6
- b) 8
- c) 10
- d) 12

QUESTION 144: The 1993 team also did something no other team had done since the 1977-78 Los Angeles Dodgers—it led the league in which of the following pairs of stats (one pitching, one offense) for a second consecutive season?
   a) ERA and runs scored
   b) ERA and homers
   c) Strikeouts and runs scored
   d) Strikeouts and homers

QUESTION 145: The Braves outscored the Marlins 22-2 during a three-game series to close out the 1999 season but won only twice, as the Marlins took the second game of the series. Bruce Chen, Kevin McGlinchy, Sean Bergman, and Darrin Ebert combined for a two-hitter in that game, but the Marlins won in ten innings. The next day, Tom Glavine and four relievers combined for a five-hit shutout as Atlanta rebounded to win its final regular season game in record fashion—the Braves set a franchise record for most runs scored during a shutout. What was the score of the Braves 1999 regular season finale?
   a) 18-0
   b) 19-0
   c) 20-0
   d) 21-0

MISCELLANEOUS

QUESTION 146: David Justice and Sid Bream scored the tying and winning runs in Game 7 of the 1992 League Championship Series when Francisco Cabrera delivered his clutch pennant-winning hit. Who was the Pirates Gold Glove outfielder that fielded the ball and nearly threw Bream out at the plate?
   a) Andy Van Slyke
   b) Barry Bonds
   c) Lloyd McClendon

QUESTION 147: The Braves have historically been strong at third base, boasting a long list of heavy hitters at the hot corner—but which third baseman was the first in franchise history to be recognized for his slick fielding with a Gold Glove?

    a) Clete Boyer

    b) Terry Pendleton

    c) Chipper Jones

QUESTION 148: And speaking of Gold Gloves . . . can you identify the player that owns the most Gold Gloves in franchise history?

    a) Dale Murphy

    b) Greg Maddux

    c) Andruw Jones

QUESTION 149: Atlanta won 95 games in 2000, becoming just the third team in baseball history to post 95-plus wins in nine consecutive seasons (non-interrupted, completed seasons). Can you identify the two teams Atlanta joined in the record book?

    a) Red Sox and Cardinals

    b) Giants and White Sox

    c) Cubs and Yankees

QUESTION 150: A member of the Braves pitching staff in 2009, this pitcher reached ten wins, 30 starts, and 150 strikeouts for the ninth consecutive season in 2008, making him the only active pitcher in baseball to accomplish that feat.

    a) Derek Lowe

    b) Javier Vazquez

    c) Kenshin Kawakami

Chapter Three Answer Key

Time to find out how you did—put a check mark next to the questions you answered correctly, and when you are done be sure and add up your score to find out your IQ, whether or not you're an All-Star, and to find out if you have a shot at making the postseason.

THE NUMBERS GAME

__ Question 101:   C – 2, in 1982 & 1983
__ Question 102:   B – 1, Andruw Jones is the only one
__ Question 103:   B – 1, at San Francisco on June 21, 1959
__ Question 104:   A – 514 and 907
__ Question 105:   C – 12

Bonus Question: Chipper Jones

THE ROOKIES

__ Question 106:   A – Eddie Mathews, in 1952
__ Question 107:   C – Earl Williams, 33, in 1971, earning Rookie of the Year honors
__ Question 108:   D – All of the above
__ Question 109:   A – Berger, he hit 38 in 1930
__ Question 110:   D – Damian Moss

THE VETERANS

__ Question 111:   D – Rico Carty
__ Question 112:   A – 0, Pendleton never won a title as a player, losing all five World Series he played in
__ Question 113:   B – Rogers Hornsby
__ Question 114:   C – Joe Adcock
__ Question 115:   D – Eddie Mathews, Hank Aaron, Joe Adcock, and Frank Thomas

THE LEGENDS
  __ Question 116:   B – Houston Astros
  __ Question 117:   A – Sam Jethroe
  __ Question 118:   B – Phil Niekro
  __ Question 119:   C – Warren Spahn
  __ Question 120:   C – Hank Aaron & Eddie Mathews

THE HITTERS
  __ Question 121:   David Justice
  __ Question 122:   Marlins, Dodgers, & Yankees
  __ Question 123:   Eddie Mathews & Hank Aaron
  __ Question 124:   Dale Murphy, 1982-85
  __ Question 125:   3, Javy Lopez, 2003, Johnny Estrada, 2004, & Brian McCann, 2006 & 2008

THE PITCHERS
  __ Question 126:   Jack Morris
  __ Question 127:   John Burkett
  __ Question 128:   Phil Niekro, 1977
  __ Question 129:   Tom Glavine, 1991-93
  __ Question 130:   Lew Burdette

THE MANAGERS AND COACHES
  __ Question 131:   D – Tim Welke
  __ Question 132:   B – John McGraw
  __ Question 133:   B – 1
  __ Question 134:   D – All of the above
  __ Question 135:   C – Glenn Hubbard

THE FABULOUS FEATS
  __ Question 136:   C – Warren Spahn & Lew Burdette
  __ Question 137:   D – Hit four home runs
  __ Question 138:   D – Rogers Hornsby, 1928
  __ Question 139:   B – Ozzie Virgil, in1987; and yes, Murphy was originally a catcher, but of these

choices, Virgil is the only one who did this feat
__ Question 140:   C – Rico Carty, 31 games in 1970

THE TEAMS

__ Question 141:   C – 1957 & 1991
__ Question 142:   A – 1948
__ Question 143:   C – 10
__ Question 144:   B – 3.14 ERA and 168 homers
__ Question 145:   A – 18-0

MISCELLANEOUS

__ Question 146:   B – Barry Bonds
__ Question 147:   A – Clete Boyer
__ Question 148:   B – Maddux won ten, Jones nine, & Murphy five
__ Question 149:   C – Cubs & Yankees
__ Question 150:   B – Javier Vazquez

Got your All-Star total? Here's how it breaks down:

STARTER WITH MOST FAN VOTES & ALL-STAR GAME MVP	= 45-50
MADE THE TEAM AND WON THE HOME RUN DERBY	= 40-44
YOU MADE IT IN THE FINAL FAN VOTE	= 35-39
YOU'RE THE GUY THAT GOT OVERLOOKED THIS YEAR	= 30-34
YOUR NUMBERS JUST AREN'T GOOD ENOUGH	= 00-29

Good luck down the stretch!

Chapter Four

DOG DAYS OF AUGUST

THE SEASON REALLY HEATS UP NOW. The Mid-Summer Classic is behind us, the trade deadline is rapidly approaching, and the race for the postseason is in full throttle. It's the Dog Days of August. This is when cagey veterans make their presence known, the weak begin to fade from contention, and that rare breed of player who just plain knows how to win—or who refuses to lose—achieves baseball immortality with his clutch exploits on the field, at the time of year when every action is magnified, and when his team and its fans need him the absolute most. Think you're that kind of player? We're about to find out . . . it's the Dog Days.

THE NUMBERS GAME

QUESTION 151: Francisco Cabrera won Game 7 of the 1992 League Championship Series with a two-out, two-run single against Pirates reliever Stan Belinda to win Atlanta's second consecutive pennant in heroic fashion. It was only his second at bat of the series. How many times did the 25-year-old first baseman/catcher bat for the Braves during the regular season?
   a)   10
   b)   83
   c)   95
   d)   137

QUESTION 152: In 1998, the club set a record for the Atlanta era of franchise history for the most consecutive games with at least one home run. Do you know how many consecutive games the

Braves hit at least one home run that season?
- a) 19
- b) 21
- c) 23
- d) 25

QUESTION 153: To follow-up on the last question, do you know how many total home runs the Braves hit during that remarkable streak?
- a) 33
- b) 38
- c) 43
- d) 48

QUESTION 154: On May 1, 1920, Boston Braves pitcher Joe Oeschger and Brooklyn Robins pitcher Leon Cadore both set a major league record for pitching the most innings in a single game. The contest ended in a 1-1 tie with both hurlers going the distance—and neither pitcher gave up a run during the final 20 innings of the game, which lasted 3:50. How many innings did Oeschger and Cadore pitch to set this remarkable record?
- a) 23
- b) 24
- c) 25
- d) 26

QUESTION 155: And to follow up on that last question . . . two Braves players that same game set a record for futility. Tony Boeckel and Charlie Pick both wore the collar at the plate that day, setting a record for most at bats in a single game without a hit—and obviously, combining for the most at bats in a single game by teammates without a hit. How many at bats did the

teammates combine for without a hit?
   a)   0 for 20
   b)   0 for 22
   c)   0 for 24
   d)   0 for 26

THE ROOKIES

QUESTION 156: Philadelphia beat Tampa to win the 2008 World Series. Philly hosted the Braves to begin 2009. In baseball history, no reigning World Series champs had ever given up a home run to a rookie who was making his first big league plate appearance—at least not until this Atlanta outfielder took Brett Myers yard on Opening Day, 2009. Can you name him?

QUESTION 157: To follow-up on that last question, prior to 2009 only one Braves rookie had ever homered in his first plate appearance with the club since the franchise moved to Atlanta in 1966—and he did it during his first major league at bat on May 17, 1996. Can you name this slugger?

QUESTION 158: And for one more follow-up question . . . later in 2009, another Braves rookie homered in his first plate appearance for the club—only this rookie did it as a pinch-hitter, and his three-run blast led Atlanta to a 9-8 victory over the Washington Nationals. It was not his first big league at bat, however, because he made 19 plate appearances with Oakland in 2008. Can you name this 29-year-old rookie infielder?

QUESTION 159: In recent years there have been some very successful NBA players who went directly from high school to the pros, skipping the collegiate ranks altogether. It is much more difficult to find success in MLB without spending time honing your skills in the minors. Can you name the Braves player who won Rookie of the Year honors after going directly from the collegiate ranks to the majors without playing a single game of minor league baseball?

QUESTION 160: Jeff Blauser set career highs with 182 hits and 110 runs in 1993, and he also became the first Braves shortstop to hit .300 in a season since 1948. Can you name the Braves *rookie* shortstop who was fourth in the league with a .322 batting average in 1948?

THE VETERANS

QUESTION 161: Dwight Evans, after 19 seasons and 2,505 games with Boston, signed as a free agent with Baltimore prior to 1991. The next time any club signed a free agent with at least 2,000 games with his original club before playing for any other team was 2009. Can you name this veteran outfielder signed by the Braves?

QUESTION 162: Javy Lopez made his first Opening Day start as the Braves catcher in 1994. Atlanta used several different players behind the plate in the years before Lopez arrived on the scene. Can you identify the veteran catcher who was the Opening Day starter for the club that won the 1991 pennant?

QUESTION 163: In 2006, Detroit won its first pennant since 1984, taking out both New York and Oakland in the postseason. The Tigers beat the Yankees in a four-game Division Series that included an intriguing pitching matchup in Game 3. The starters that day were Randy Johnson for the Yankees and Kenny Rogers for the Tigers. It was only the second time in baseball history that opposing starters in a postseason game had both pitched in at least 500 regular season games. The first time that happened was one year earlier when the Braves met the Astros in the 2005 Division Series. Can you name the veteran starters who combined had pitched 1,307 career games prior to taking the mound for Houston and Atlanta during Game 2 of the 2005 Division Series?

QUESTION 164: Think about the group of guys that were the nucleus of the "worst-to-first" 1991 club. Only one player was on both ends of the 14 consecutive division titles, playing for the 1991 and 2005 clubs. Can you name this veteran?

QUESTION 165: Atlanta acquired veteran slugger Gary Sheffield from the Dodgers via a trade prior to the 2002 season. In return the Dodgers got three players: Odalis Perez, Andrew Brown, and this guy, a veteran slugger and a former All-Star in his own right. Can you name the Braves outfielder included in the trade for Sheffield?

THE LEGENDS

QUESTION 166: The Braves franchise boasts a very long list of quality hitters who suited it up for the team, but despite that, only one Brave in the 20th century claimed two batting titles for the club. Can you name the legend who was a two-time batting champion?

QUESTION 167: On July 14, 1978, umpire Doug Harvey tossed this veteran pitcher after discovering he intentionally scuffed up three balls during a game in which he was gunning for his 200th career victory. This pitcher later joined the very exclusive 300-wins club . . . and for a second career he became a very popular announcer for your Atlanta Braves. Can you name this legendary Hall of Famer?

QUESTION 168: Atlanta lost 4-3 to the Houston Astros on May 29, 1976. In that game fans witnessed a baseball first—one pitcher hit the only home run of his big league career against his brother, who he beat on the mound that day and obviously at the plate as well. Name the former Braves pitcher who beat Atlanta that day with his pitching and offense. He remains the only player in history to hit his only career home run against his brother.

QUESTION 169: Bobby Murcer once said, "Trying to hit him is like trying to eat Jell-O with chopsticks." Which Braves legend was Murcer referring to when he made that remark?

QUESTION 170: Stan Musial once remarked, jokingly, that this Braves legend would never be in the Hall of Fame because "he'll never stop pitching." The player he was referring to was more than just a baseball hero—he also won the Purple Heart and a Bronze Star while serving in the military during World War II. Can you name him?

THE HITTERS

QUESTION 171: Talk about a torrid start to a season—at the conclusion of play on May 26, 1959, Hank Aaron was batting .442 with 72 hits, 13 homers, and 44 RBI. The Braves had only played 39 games at that point. Aaron had only played 38 games. From 1960-2008, only four National League players collected at least 60 hits and ten home runs in fewer than 40 team games to start the season: Billy Williams (1964 Cubs), Lou Brock (1967 Cardinals), Larry Walker (1997 Rockies), and . . . this star, who did it for Atlanta. Can you name him?

QUESTION 172: According to the Elias Sports Bureau, there are only two players in all of baseball history who began their careers with as many as 14 consecutive seasons with at least 20 homers—and both of them played for the Braves. Can you name these record-setting sluggers?

QUESTION 173: On July 1, 2009, Alex Rodriguez and Ken Griffey, Jr. both homered in the Mariners vs. Yankees matchup at the new Yankee Stadium. The Elias Sports Bureau reported that it was only the second time in baseball history that two players with at least 550 career homers went yard in the same contest—the first time was 1971 in a Braves vs. Giants matchup. Can you name the legendary sluggers who did it back then?

QUESTION 174: Chipper Jones did it, and so did Dale Murphy and Hank Aaron. What is *it* exactly that we're talking about here? Back-to-back 30-homer seasons, that's what—and it isn't as easy as it sounds. Can you name the Braves old-timer who became the first player in franchise history to post consecutive 30-homer campaigns?

QUESTION 175: And speaking of power . . . can you name the first player in franchise history to launch 40 homers in a single season?

THE PITCHERS

QUESTION 176: It was pitching that carried the Braves to a second consecutive division title in 1992, and it was pitching that carried the club to the pennant as well. One Braves starter was 2-0 vs. Pittsburgh in the 1992 League Championship Series. He struck out 19 batters, posted a 2.66 earned run average, and was named Series MVP. Can you identify this pitcher?
   a) Steve Avery
   b) Tom Glavine
   c) John Smoltz
   d) Pete Smith

QUESTION 177: Warren Spahn, who was a 14-time All-Star, placed among the top three in Cy Young balloting five times in six seasons from 1956-61. He also set a major league record when he led the league in the same two categories for five consecutive seasons. Which two categories did Spahn lead the league every

season from 1957-61?
a) Wins and earned run average
b) Earned run average and complete games
c) Strikeouts and earned run average
d) Wins and complete games

QUESTION 178: Carl Morton was fifth among league leaders with four shutouts in 1973, his first season with the Braves, including a 1-0 victory vs. Houston on July 3. The way Morton notched his shutout that day was so unusual that the Braves staff has repeated the feat only once since then, a 2-0 victory vs. Chicago on June 22, 2009. What was so unusual about Morton's shutout?
a) He gave up five extra-base hits
b) He did not strikeout a single batter
c) He gave up ten hits, all singles
d) He walked seven batters

QUESTION 179: Tom Glavine once said, "I think when you are around great players, they make you better." Who was he referring to when he made that statement?
a) John Smoltz
b) Greg Maddux
c) Chipper Jones
d) Hank Aaron

QUESTION 180: Among pitchers with at least 1,000 innings for the Braves, which of the following posted the highest ratio of strikeouts per nine innings? The ratio is a very impressive 7.98 Ks per nine innings pitched wearing a Braves uniform.
a) Kevin Millwood
b) Steve Avery
c) John Smoltz
d) Phil Niekro

THE MANAGERS AND COACHES

QUESTION 181: On April 12, 1955, the Milwaukee Braves trailed the Cincinnati Reds 2-1 in the eighth inning when a 25-year-old rookie outfielder pinch-hit for Warren Spahn in the first at bat of his big league career. The rookie wasted no time, launching a game-tying homer on the very first pitch and sparking a three-run rally that gave Spahn and the Braves a 4-2 victory in their first game of the season. That outfielder hit only 21 career homers, but he was the first player in history to hit a pinch-hit homer in his first big league at bat and he later won 2,738 games and one world championship as a big league manager—and he won 153 games managing the Braves. Can you name this legendary skipper?

QUESTION 182: On July 15, 1978, this current (2009) Braves coach helped turn a triple play for Atlanta vs. the Philadelphia Phillies . . . in only his *second* big league game. Can you name him?

QUESTION 183: He was the Braves bullpen coach twice, in 1985 and from 1988-90, and in 2007 he began his third stint with the club—this time coaching third base. Who is he?

QUESTION 184: A third-round draft pick for the New York Mets in 1982, he won a World Series with the Mets in 1986. He joined the Braves coaching staff in 2006. Can you name him?

QUESTION 185: Long before his successful coaching career with the Braves, he was one of the most pivotal free agent signings for General Manager John Schuerholz and he earned Comeback Player of the Year honors in his first season in Atlanta. Can you name him?

THE FABULOUS FEATS

QUESTION 186: Four players hit for the cycle for the Braves franchise during the 20th century, but only one player did it after the club moved to Atlanta—and there was a gap in excess of 75 years between the club's third and fourth cycle. Can you name the switch-hitting outfielder who hit for the cycle vs. Houston on September 23, 1987, despite hitting only five career homers?

QUESTION 187: Atlanta's 13-game winning streak in July, 1992, that catapulted the club into first place, was capped off with a 1-0 victory vs. Pittsburgh on July 25. The Braves offense managed only one hit that day, but it was a solo home run by David Justice. Charlie Leibrandt, Alejandro Pena, and Kent Mercker combined on a five-hitter for Atlanta—but it took a spectacular ninth-inning catch to preserve the shutout. "I was in a daze. That's the best play I ever saw," said David Justice, after one of his teammates robbed the Pirates Andy Van Slyke of a two-run ninth-inning homer. Can you name the outfielder who performed this fabulous feat? The *New York Times* described it this way: "[He] was in full stride when he leaped on the padded ten-foot fence and reached over it for the game-saving catch."

QUESTION 188: On May 26, 1959, Pirates pitcher Harvey Haddix tossed 12 perfect innings against the Braves, but lost his perfect game, no-hitter, shutout, and the contest in the 13th. Haddix gave up only one hit and one unearned run, but Atlanta won 1-0 thanks to this pitcher, who scattered 12 hits while tossing 13 shutout innings for the complete game victory—can you name the Braves starter who upended Haddix and the Pirates?

QUESTION 189: Imagine being the first player in all of baseball history to accomplish a fabulous feat. That's exactly what one Braves player did with these numbers: .319 average, 45 homers, 41 doubles, 110 RBI, 116 runs, 126 walks, and 25 steals. No one else in history had ever batted above .300 with 40 homers and

40 doubles, while hitting the century mark in RBI, runs, and walks, and stealing 20 bases. Can you name the player that did it for Atlanta?

QUESTION 190: Since the club moved to Atlanta in 1966, the franchise record for most two-homer games in one season is eight. Imagine hitting two bombs in a game *eight* times in one season—that's pretty amazing. Two different players have done it for the Braves, one in 1998 and the other in 2003 . . . and you have to come up with both names to get this one right. Can you name the two Braves players who had eight two-homer games in one season?

BONUS QUESTION: Which future Braves outfielder became the first person to ever hit a major league home run and score an NFL touchdown during the same week? His second big league homer, it came on September 5, 1989, and just five days later he scored his first career NFL touchdown.

THE TEAMS

You know Atlanta set a professional sports record by winning 14 consecutive division titles from 1991-2005, but how well do you know Braves team trivia from that remarkable run? Here are five questions about those teams to help settle the issue.

QUESTION 191: Billy Wagner struck out Miguel Cabrera to preserve the Mets 6-4 victory vs. the Florida Marlins on September 12, 2006, and with that win for New York, Atlanta was eliminated from division title contention and its streak of 14 consecutive division crowns came to an end. The winning pitcher for New York was Guillermo Mota. Nearly 15 years earlier, on October 5, 1991, it was a Dodgers loss at San Francisco, combined with a Braves victory vs. Houston that began Atlanta's remarkable run. Can you name the Braves Young Gun who was the winning pitcher against the Astros on October 5, 1991?

QUESTION 192: Atlanta hit the century mark in victories six times during its record postseason run, including a stretch of three consecutive seasons at one point. The highest victory total during the Braves 14-year playoff run was 106, and it came in the second of those three consecutive seasons in which the club hit the century mark. In what year did the Braves win 106 games to run away with yet another division crown?

QUESTION 193: The Braves beat the Dodgers by a single game to win the 1991 N.L. West title—and two years later Atlanta made it three straight titles by outlasting the Giants in a thrilling race by a single game. After moving to the N.L. East, the closest any team got to catching the Braves was the 2000 Mets, who also lost by a single game. The norm was double-digits, with the largest margin of victory being 21 games over two teams that tied for second—the Mets and Phillies—despite the fact Atlanta won only 90 games that season. In what year did the Braves win only 90 games, and yet . . . Atlanta still won the division title by 21 games over the Mets and Phillies?

QUESTION 194: Atlanta won the pennant in 1991, the same season it began its 14-year postseason run—but exactly how many times in 14 seasons did the Braves go on to win the N.L. pennant?

QUESTION 195: Atlanta won the 1995 World Series, but the other 13 postseasons ended in heartache with a disappointing loss. How many times did the Braves lose a playoff series in a winner-take-all deciding game (either Game 5 of a Division Series or Game 7 of the League Championship Series or World Series)?

MISCELLANEOUS

QUESTION 196: The Braves have boasted their fair share of outstanding outfielders through the years—but can you name the very first Gold Glove outfielder in franchise history? If it helps, he won the award three times—all consecutively.

QUESTION 197: Greg Maddux left Atlanta as the franchise leader in winning percentage and earned run average, and during his tenure with the club he was known to favor a specific catcher when he took the mound. Can you name the Braves catcher who caught Maddux more than any other?

QUESTION 198: He led the USA Junior National Team to a world championship in 1998, he was *Baseball America's* top high school prospect in 2001, the Gatorade National High School Player of the Year in 2001, and after he was signed by his father, a major league scout, he was named the Angels top rated prospect by *Baseball America* three times (2002, 2004, and 2005). Not a bad resume. He joined the Braves in 2008—can you name this player?

QUESTION 199: Buzz Capra led the league with a 2.29 earned run average in 1974, but it took nearly 20 years before another Braves hurler posted the best number in the league. Can you name the pitcher who did just that in 1993?

QUESTION 200: Legendary Braves broadcasters Skip Caray, Pete Van Wieren, and Ernie Johnson brought thousands of games to life for an entire generation of radio listeners and viewers of TBS. Skip and Pete began broadcasting for the Braves the same season—do you know what year it was?

Chapter Four Answer Key

Time to find out how you did—put a check mark next to the questions you answered correctly, and when you are done be sure and add up your score to find out your IQ, and . . . most importantly, how you did down the stretch.

THE NUMBERS GAME
- __ Question 151:   A – 10
- __ Question 152:   D – 25
- __ Question 153:   C – 43
- __ Question 154:   D – 26
- __ Question 155:   B – 0 for 22

THE ROOKIES
- __ Question 156:   Jordan Schafer
- __ Question 157:   Jermaine Dye
- __ Question 158:   Brooks Conrad
- __ Question 159:   Bob Horner, 1978
- __ Question 160:   Alvin Dark

THE VETERANS
- __ Question 161:   Garret Anderson
- __ Question 162:   Mike Heath
- __ Question 163:   Roger Clemens & John Smoltz
- __ Question 164:   John Smoltz, he was the last holdover from 1991 when he left Atlanta after 2008
- __ Question 165:   Brian Jordan

THE LEGENDS
- __ Question 166:   Hank Aaron, 1956 & 1959
- __ Question 167:   Don Sutton
- __ Question 168:   Joe Niekro
- __ Question 169:   Phil Niekro
- __ Question 170:   Warren Spahn

THE HITTERS
___ Question 171:   Chipper Jones, 2008
___ Question 172:   Eddie Mathews & Chipper Jones (Hank Aaron only hit 13 as a rookie, but then hit 20 or more the next 20 seasons)
___ Question 173:   Hank Aaron & Willie Mays
___ Question 174:   Wally Berger, 1934-35
___ Question 175:   Eddie Mathews

THE PITCHERS
___ Question 176:   C – John Smoltz
___ Question 177:   D – Wins and complete games, and he actually led the league in complete games seven consecutive seasons, 1957-63
___ Question 178:   C – He gave up ten hits, all singles
___ Question 179:   B – Greg Maddux
___ Question 180:   C – John Smoltz

THE MANAGERS AND COACHES
___ Question 181:   Chuck Tanner
___ Question 182:   Glenn Hubbard
___ Question 183:   Brian Snitker
___ Question 184:   Roger McDowell
___ Question 185:   Terry Pendleton

THE FABULOUS FEATS
___ Question 186:   Albert Hall
___ Question 187:   Otis Nixon
___ Question 188:   Lew Burdette
___ Question 189:   Chipper Jones, during his 1999 MVP season
___ Question 190:   Andres Galarraga, 1998, & Javy Lopez, 2003

Bonus Question: Deion Sanders

THE TEAMS

__ Question 191:   John Smoltz
__ Question 192:   1998
__ Question 193:   1995
__ Question 194:   5
__ Question 195:   4, 1991 World Series, 2002-04 Division
                   Series

MISCELLANEOUS

__ Question 196:   Hank Aaron, 1958-60
__ Question 197:   Eddie Perez
__ Question 198:   Casey Kotchman
__ Question 199:   Greg Maddux
__ Question 200:   1976

Got your Dog Days total? Here's how it breaks down:

WON THE PENNANT AND NLCS MVP HONORS	= 45-50
WON THE PENNANT IN A THRILLING SEVEN-GAME SERIES	= 40-44
DIVISION CHAMPION	= 35-39
LATE SEASON SLUMP BUT YOU GOT THE WILD CARD	= 30-34
SITTING HOME THIS OCTOBER	= 00-29

Good luck in October!

Chapter Five

OCTOBER BASEBALL

IT ALL COMES DOWN TO THIS. You spent your childhood dreaming of this moment.

It's October baseball.

This is your one chance at baseball immortality. You're the underdog. No one expected you to make it this far, but at least to this point you've proved them all wrong. The only thing left to prove is that you have what it takes to be a world champion. No need to be nervous—it's not like we saved the 50 toughest questions for last or anything.

THE NUMBERS GAME

QUESTION 201: The Chicago Cubs set a major league record in 2006 for the most consecutive games at the start of a season in which the club hit at least one first-inning homer. Atlanta tied that record in 2009 thanks to a first-inning blast by catcher Brian McCann (his second of the season). In how many consecutive games did Atlanta hit a first-inning homer at the start of 2009?

QUESTION 202: Only one player in franchise history has ever worn the name of his hometown on the back of his jersey . . . as his jersey number. His name was Bill Voiselle and he was from a rural town in South Carolina—a town that had a number for its name. What was the jersey number (and hometown) of Voiselle, a veteran pitcher who won 28 games during parts of three seasons with the club?

QUESTION 203: Andy Messersmith was twice a 20-game winner, a four-time All-Star, a two-time Gold Glove recipient, and the Cy Young runner-up for the Dodgers in 1974, prior to signing a free agent contract with Atlanta in 1976. Since owner Ted Turner was spending big bucks to get the pitcher to Atlanta, he figured a little ploy to get the most out of his money was well within his rights . . . and so instead of the name "Messersmith" on the back of his jersey, the Braves new hurler wore the name "Channel" with his number directly beneath it—and of course, his jersey number corresponded perfectly with Turner's TV station, WTBS. The league forced Turner to stop using Messersmith to plug WTBS, but can you name the jersey (station) number worn by Messersmith as part of Turner's creative ad campaign?

QUESTION 204: And speaking of jersey numbers, in 1978, Atlanta actually banned its players at all levels from wearing one number in particular. Any idea what number it was?

QUESTION 205: Tommie Aaron hit a career high eight homers as a rookie for the Braves in 1962, and on June 12, that same season, he and brother Hank Aaron both homered in the same contest vs. the Dodgers. Bobby and Barry Bonds hold the major league record for career homers for a father and son, but the Aaron brothers hold the record for career homers by brothers. How many home runs did Tommie and Hank Aaron combine for during their respective playing careers?

THE ROOKIES

QUESTION 206: In 2005, Atlanta became the first team in baseball history to reach the postseason with five rookies who all had 100-plus at bats during the regular season. No other team had made the postseason with more than four such rookies. Two of the Braves rookies in 2005 who batted 100-plus times were Wilson Betemit and Pete Orr. Can you name the other three?

QUESTION 207: In 2005, this player was rated the overall #3 prospect in the Braves organization, and he proved why that was the case when he made his big league debut in June, 2007, batting .326 with 104 hits in 94 games. He also batted .336 that season after the All-Star break, which was the second highest average in the league among all rookies. A native of Cuba, can you name this player?

QUESTION 208: In June, 2008, this Braves rookie posted a 3-0 record with a 1.63 earned run average in four starts—and for those numbers he earned Gillette's Rookie of the Month honors for the National League. He received a trophy, as well as a $5,000 donation to a charity of his choice . . . who was this Braves rookie?

QUESTION 209: In June, 2009, this Braves rookie posted a 4-0 record with a 2.48 earned run average in five starts—two of his victories came in back-to-back starts vs. the Yankees and Red Sox—and for those numbers he earned National League Rookie of the Month honors . . . who was this Braves rookie?

QUESTION 210: It took 131 plate appearances before the Braves rookie who made this statement earned his first big league walk: "The moment I start looking for a walk is when a fastball goes right down the middle, and then I'd be kicking myself." Who was this free-swinger?

THE VETERANS

QUESTION 211: All of these players have something in common: Charlie Kerfeld, Doug Sisk, Ernie Whitt, Jeff Parrett, Jim Presley, Jim Vatcher, Kevin Batiste, Mark Grant, Marvin Freeman, Rico Rossy, Tommy Hinzo, and Victor Rosario. Atlanta acquired all nine players via trade prior to or during the 1990 season. Can you identify the three players the Braves received for trading

veteran outfielder and fan-favorite Dale Murphy?
   a)   Mark Grant, Charlie Kerfeld, and Doug Sisk
   b)   Ernie Whitt, Jim Presley, and Kevin Batiste
   c)   Marvin Freeman, Rico Rossy, and Tommy Hinzo
   d)   Victor Rosario, Jeff Parrett, and Jim Vatcher

QUESTION 212: Branch Rickey once told Pirates Hall of Famer Ralph Kiner, "We finished last with you and we could have finished last without you." There have been more than a few great players on some otherwise really bad Braves teams, as well. One such veteran won two-thirds of the Triple Crown in 1935 and started in the All-Star Game for a Braves club that was 38-115 on the season. Who was this veteran star?
   a)   Shanty Hogan
   b)   Rabbit Maranville
   c)   Buck Jordan
   d)   Wally Berger

QUESTION 213: To follow-up on that theme of players who put up great numbers for really bad teams, Atlanta's only All-Star representative in 1988 batted .300 with a .400 slugging percentage for a Braves club that finished 54-106. Who was this veteran?
   a)   Dale Murphy
   b)   Gerald Perry
   c)   Andres Thomas
   d)   Dion James

QUESTION 214: The Cardinals Jim Edmonds struck out four times during a game in 2006 in which none of his teammates struck out even once. Bad enough to go down on strikes four times, but to have none of your teammate's strikeout at all, well, that's a pretty rough night at the plate. That kind of night, thankfully, is pretty rare. In fact, the last time a major league player had that dubious honor was more than 20 years earlier . . . and he did it

for the Braves. Who was this veteran?
 a) Dale Murphy
 b) Bob Horner
 c) Rafael Ramirez
 d) Gerald Perry

QUESTION 215: Bobby Abreu (ten hits, seven walks for the Yankees) and Manny Ramirez (eight hits, nine walks for the Red Sox) both reached base 17 times during a five-game series between the Yankees and Red Sox in 2006. That's getting the job done. In fact, no one in baseball had reached base that many times in one series in more than 20 years . . . the last being a Braves veteran who collected ten hits and seven walks during a five-game series vs. LA in 1985. Which Braves veteran lit up a Dodgers pitching staff that was the best in the league that season?
 a) Dale Murphy
 b) Terry Harper
 c) Claudell Washington
 d) Gerald Perry

THE LEGENDS

QUESTION 216: Dick Williams once called this Hall of Famer's signature pitch, ". . . unhittable, unless he hangs it, and he never does. It's worse than trying to hit a knuckleball." Name the pitcher . . . and his signature pitch.

QUESTION 217: He hit 398 career homers, all but 27 for the Braves—can you name this slugger?

QUESTION 218: In 2009, Chipper Jones moved ahead of this Braves legend and into second place in the franchise record book for career RBI—which Braves legend did Jones overtake in 2009?

QUESTION 219: To follow-up on that last question, Chipper is one of five players to drive in more than 1,000 runs for the Braves. Can you name the other four?

QUESTION 220: On July 2, 1963, Juan Marichal pitched a 16-inning complete game shutout vs. the Braves. Marichal said, "I begged Mr. Dark [Giants manager] to let me stay a few more inning, and he did. In the 12th or 13th, he wanted to take me out, and I said, 'Please, please, let me stay.' Then in the 14th, he said, 'No more for you,' and I said, 'Do you see that man on the mound?' . . . 'That man is 42, and I'm 25. I'm not ready for you to take me out.'" Who was the 42-year-old veteran pitcher for the Braves that day? He tossed 15-plus scoreless innings before Willie Mays hit a walk-off homer in the 16th to give Marichal the 1-0 victory in one of the most memorable regular season games in history.

THE HITTERS

QUESTION 221: Atlanta was the only team in baseball with three Silver Slugger recipients in 2003. It was the fifth consecutive season for one, but it was his first with the Braves. It was the third Silver Slugger for another, but all three came for different teams. And for the third player, it was the only Silver Slugger of his career. Can you name the three Braves who won Silver Slugger Awards in 2003?

QUESTION 222: Atlanta led the league in several offensive categories in 1973: 799 runs, .266 average, .339 on-base percentage, .427 slugging percentage, and 206 home runs. Hank Aaron hit 40 homers that season, but his total was only third best on the club as the Braves boasted three players with 40-plus homers. Can you name the two infielders who also hit 40-plus homers that season for Atlanta?

QUESTION 223: Atlanta won 88 games in 1974, but placed only third in the division race. The team could pitch (second fewest earned runs allowed in the league) but struggled at the plate (third worst batting average in the league). The offense might have struggled, but at season's end it was a Braves outfielder who won the batting title (.353) and led the league in hits (214). Can you name the All-Star outfielder who won the 1974 batting title?

QUESTION 224: David Justice led the Braves with 120 RBI in 1993, but he was joined by two teammates who also hit the century mark in RBI: Ron Gant (117) and Fred McGriff (101). It was the first time since 1970 that three N.L. teammates hit the century mark in RBI . . . and coincidentally, it was three Braves who did it in 1970 as well. Can you name the Braves trio that all surpassed 100 RBI in 1970?

QUESTION 225: Pirates Hall of Famer Paul Waner set a major league record in 1927 for most consecutive games with an extra-base hit. His record was tied in 2006 by Braves future Hall of Famer Chipper Jones, who went nine consecutive games without an extra-base hit before catching fire on June 26, when he was 3 for 4 with a home run against the Yankees. Jones hit seven homers, eight doubles, and one triple during his record-tying streak—16 extra-base hits, but do you know in how many consecutive games Jones got at least one extra-base hit?

BONUS QUESTION: To follow-up on Chipper Jones, through 2009 he is one of only six switch-hitters in baseball history to pick up 1,000 or more RBI for one team. Can you come up with the other five switch-hitters to reach that milestone with one club? Here's some help: as of 2009, one of them is still active and two of them are members of the Hall of Fame.

THE PITCHERS

QUESTION 226: Atlanta was in need of bullpen help when it acquired reliever Bob Wickman from the Cleveland Indians in July, 2006. Wickman took over as closer and converted his first 11 save opportunities for the Braves. It was the third time since 1991 that a Braves acquisition converted at least ten consecutive saves after joining the club. Kyle Farnsworth saved ten straight in 2005. Can you name the closer who went 11 for 11 down the stretch for the 1991 division champs?

QUESTION 227: On September 11, 1991, three Atlanta Braves pitchers combined to no-hit the San Diego Padres. Can you name all three pitchers?

QUESTION 228: Atlanta became renowned for its pitching staff in the 1990s . . . but can you name the pitcher who got the nod on Opening Day for Atlanta five times from 1982-88?

QUESTION 229: On April 12, 2009, Mets ace Johan Santana posted this line *vs.* the Florida Marlins: 7 IP, 3 H, 0 ER, *and 13 K.* Only problem, well, he was the losing pitcher in a 2-1 decision against Marlins starter Josh Johnson. In the previous 35 seasons of major league baseball there was only one instance of a player striking out 13 batters, not allowing an earned run, and *still* going on record as the losing pitcher. And he pitched for Atlanta. This 23-year-old hurler was only 5-14 in 1989, and on April 15, he lost to the Giants 2-0 despite posting this line: 8 IP, 3 H, 0 ER, *and 13 K.* Can you name this Braves hard-luck loser?

QUESTION 230: The Braves were in last place on May 27, 1992—but that quickly changed as the club got exceptionally hot, and the fortunes of the club were directly tied to its pitching staff. The Young Gun who got the win on May 27 snapped a personal two-game skid, but he didn't stop there. He reeled off a modern day franchise record 13 consecutive victories, closing out his run with a complete game on August 19 vs. Montreal. Atlanta was in last place, seven games behind the Giants when his streak began, but after 13 consecutive wins by this starter the Braves were in first place, 6.5 games ahead of Cincinnati . . . can you name this ace?

THE MANAGERS AND COACHES

QUESTION 231: Atlanta placed fifth in its division after winning just 76 games in 1973. The Braves were managed that season by a former player who was a nine-time All-Star. It was his second year at the helm and his only full season as manager, as he was replaced by Clyde King during the 1974 season. Can you come up with the name of the Braves skipper during the 1973 season?

QUESTION 232: In 1983, while with the Philadelphia Phillies, he became the first manager in history to be fired by a team that was in first place. After managing in Texas, Philly, and Cleveland, in 1990 he began a long tenure as bench coach for the Braves. Can you come up with his name?

QUESTION 233: A former school teacher who decided to attend a major league tryout camp, he was signed as an amateur free agent in 1966 by the Pittsburgh Pirates and he eventually pitched 11 seasons in the majors, including a brief stint with the Braves from 1975-76. Later he became a highly respected coach. He was the Braves pitching coach from 1987-90, and beginning in 1991 the man called DC by nearly everyone in the Braves organization began a long tenure as a minor league instructor for the club. Can you name this coach?

QUESTION 234: After playing basketball and baseball for Georgia Tech, he spent time playing and managing in the minors for the St. Louis Cardinals organization. He began his coaching career with the Braves in 1974. He retired as bullpen coach after 2006, but continued working in a variety of roles with the club. In

2008, he began his 35th consecutive season with the organization, and in 2009 he marked his overall 50th major league spring training. Who is this legendary Braves coach?

QUESTION 235: Previously he was best known for being the first American to win a home run title in Japan (he actually won two years in a row, 1974-75), but after David Justice said, "He made a big impact on me . . . he keeps me on track," this Braves hitting coach gained far greater recognition among Braves fans. Can you name him?

THE FABULOUS FEATS

QUESTION 236: No doubt Francisco Cabrera's clutch hit and Sid Bream's agonizingly slow, painful dash for the plate is one of the most enduring and recognizable images in Braves history. After all, that heroic ninth-inning rally won the pennant. You know Bobby Cox and Jim Leyland were the managers that day for Atlanta and Pittsburgh. You know Dough Drabek was the starter that baffled Braves bats all day long, and you know it was Stan Belinda who gave up the two-out hit to Cabrera. You might even remember that the home plate umpire was Randy Marsh. Well, how about this one . . . who was the Braves third base coach that day? You know, the one waving Bream to the plate.

QUESTION 237: On April 13, 1987, the Padres Marvell Wynne, Tony Gwynn, and John Kruk became the first teammates in history to begin a game with three consecutive homers (oddly enough, those three comprised the Padres outfield, but San Diego went on to lose the game 13-6 at home to the Giants). Jeff Austin was the starting pitcher for the Cincinnati Reds at Turner Field on May 28, 2003, when the Braves offense became the second team in history to hit three consecutive homers to start a game (incidentally, Javy Lopez added a fourth homer later in the inning as the Braves rolled to a 15-3 win). Rafael Furcal hit the leadoff homer and Gary Sheffield hit the third straight solo shot. Can you name the Braves infielder who hit the second of those three consecutive blasts?

QUESTION 238: Gene Conley was on the 1957 Milwaukee Braves club that won the World Series. He also won three NBA championship titles (the pitcher stood six-foot-eight) and became the first (and so far only) athlete in history to play for three different sports franchises in the same city. At the very least you should be able to name the city where he pulled off this remarkable feat . . . but can you also name the three franchises?

QUESTION 239: Do you remember Morganna Roberts? You might know her better as the exotic dancer who became baseball's "kissing bandit." She frequently rushed players on the field and planted (much to the delight of fans . . . and probably players, too) rather enthusiastic kisses on the guys she singled out. She got the Braves third baseman on August 31, 1969, and would you believe her charm busted him from a prolonged slump? He was mired in a 1 for 17 drought but after the kiss he was 3 for 4 that day and reached base safely in eight of his next 15 plate appearances. He also won his only career Gold Glove that season—can you name this Braves third baseman?

QUESTION 240: Atlanta won the 1995 World Series—you know that—but did you know that one of the Braves players did something in that series that no other player in baseball history had ever done before? Games 3, 4, and 5 were all on the road in Cleveland, and yet one Braves player hit a homer in all three of those road games. It was the first time in history a player homered in three consecutive road games in a single World Series. Can you name the slugger who did this for Atlanta in 1995?

THE TEAMS

QUESTION 241: Atlanta won 88 games in 1974, but only placed third in the N.L. West, 14 games behind the Dodgers. The Braves actually had a losing record against six teams, including LA, and played .500 or better against only five teams in the league. The Braves, however, did set a major league record for the most consecutive wins against one opponent since divisional play began in 1969. Atlanta won 15 consecutive games and was 17-1 overall against this club. Can you name the division rival that Atlanta completely dominated in 1974?

QUESTION 242: Atlanta was only 38-40 after the 1982 All-Star break, but still held on to win its division by a single game over the Dodgers and two games over the Giants. The Braves won the West thanks in part to a record-setting winning streak out of the gate. How many consecutive games did the Braves win to start the 1982 season?

QUESTION 243: Bobby Cox managed the club to its 14th consecutive division title in 2005, and he did it with contributions from an unbelievable number of rookies. This was not a veteran team, and the managerial job done by Cox led many to proclaim that season his finest ever at the helm. Atlanta lost a heartbreaker in the Division Series when the Astros Chris Burke hit an extra-inning homer against Braves rookie Joey Devine to win Game 4 and the series. How many rookies did Bobby Cox and the Braves use in 2005, and how many innings did Game 4 vs. Houston last? It's the same number.

QUESTION 244: The 1997 club was the first to play its home games at Turner Field. Atlanta's first home game that season was on April 4, and it was a 5-4 victory vs. the Cubs. The Braves pounded out 15 hits that day, but only one of them left the park. Can you recall which player hit the first regular season home run in Turner Field history?

QUESTION 245: The Braves offense in 2003 was the best in the league—by a long shot. The club led the league in runs, hits, homers, average, slugging, OPS, and total bases, and in the process set a franchise record for team home runs. Six players hit 20 or more bombs for the Braves that season—and in fact, I was at an interleague game in Tampa when the Braves pregame batting practice was so impressive, bomb after bomb hitting the back wall of The Trop, that it was the number one topic discussed that night on the Rays postgame radio program. How many total homers did the Braves launch in 2003?

MISCELLANEOUS

QUESTION 246: Del Crandall won four Gold Gloves in five seasons from 1958-62. He also made four of his eight career All-Star teams during that same stretch. What position did Crandall play when he won all that hardware?

QUESTION 247: Who was the first player in franchise history other than Crandall to win a Gold Glove at that position? Also a perennial All-Star, and later an MVP recipient, this player is better known for his managerial success.

QUESTION 248: Talk about a ticket stub you'd want to keep . . . on August 10, 2003, the Braves lost a tough 3-2 decision on the road in St. Louis when Albert Pujols went yard against John Smoltz in the eighth inning. You hate to lose, but seeing Smoltz and Pujols going head-to-head with the game on the line was worth the price of admission. Oh, and in that same game, for the first time in franchise history a Braves player turned an unassisted triple play. It was voted MLB.com "Play of the Year" and was turned in by . . . which Braves infielder?

QUESTION 249: After Senator George Mitchell released the report of his 20-month performance enhancing drugs investigation, a former Braves player said: "It's disappointing and discouraging, but this is the moment baseball has been waiting for to shock us into action . . . it's an opportunity I hope baseball doesn't miss. We can still change the culture of baseball." Do you know which Braves player made these remarks? He backs them up too, seeing as he started the I Won't Cheat Foundation to help young students all across the country make good choices when it comes to school, sports, playing by the rules, and using performance enhancing drugs.

QUESTION 250: Atlanta won the 1992 pennant in a thrilling seven-game series vs. the Pittsburgh Pirates, despite the fact one Pirates pitcher tossed two complete game victories vs. the Braves in that series. It was the first (and through 2008, only) time in modern history that one pitcher notched a pair of complete game victories in a single postseason series vs. the Braves. Who was it that gave the Braves offense so much trouble during the 1992 NLCS?

Chapter Five Answer Key

Time to find out how you did—put a check mark next to the questions you answered correctly, and when you are done be sure and add up your score to find out your IQ, and whether or not you've earned a world championship ring.

THE NUMBERS GAME
__ Question 201:   3
__ Question 202:   Ninety-Six, or 96
__ Question 203:   17
__ Question 204:   13
__ Question 205:   768, but only 13 for Tommie

THE ROOKIES
__ Question 206:   Kelly Johnson, Jeff Francoeur, and Brian McCann
__ Question 207:   Yunel Escobar
__ Question 208:   Jair Jurrjens
__ Question 209:   Tommy Hanson
__ Question 210:   Jeff Francoeur

THE VETERANS
__ Question 211:   D – Victor Rosario, Jeff Parrett, and Jim Vatcher
__ Question 212:   D – Wally Berger
__ Question 213:   B – Gerald Perry
__ Question 214:   A – Dale Muprhy
__ Question 215:   A – Dale Murphy

THE LEGENDS
__ Question 216:   Bruce Sutter, split-finger fastball
__ Question 217:   Dale Murphy
__ Question 218:   Eddie Mathews

__ Question 219:   Hank Aaron, Eddie Mathews, Dale
                   Murphy, & Andruw Jones
__ Question 220:   Warren Spahn

THE HITTERS

__ Question 221:   Mike Hampton, Gary Sheffield, & Javy
                   Lopez
__ Question 222:   Davey Johnson, 43, & Darrell Evans, 41
__ Question 223:   Ralph Garr
__ Question 224:   Hank Aaron, Orlando Cepeda, and Rico
                   Carty
__ Question 225:   14

Bonus Question: Mickey Mantle (Yankees), Bernie Williams
                (Yankees), Eddie Murray (Orioles), Pete
                Rose (Reds), Lance Berkman (Astros)

THE PITCHERS

__ Question 226:   Alejandro Pena
__ Question 227:   Kent Mercker, Mark Wohlers, & Alejandro
                   Pena
__ Question 228:   Rick Mahler
__ Question 229:   Pete Smith
__ Question 230:   Tom Glavine

THE MANAGERS AND COACHES

__ Question 231:   Eddie Mathews
__ Question 232:   Pat Corrales
__ Question 233:   Bruce Dal Canton
__ Question 234:   Bobby Dews
__ Question 235:   Clarence Jones

THE FABULOUS FEATS

__ Question 236:   Jimy Williams
__ Question 237:   Mark DeRosa
__ Question 238:   Boston: Celtics, Red Sox, & Braves

_ Question 239:   Clete Boyer
_ Question 240:   Ryan Klesko

THE TEAMS
_ Question 241:   San Diego Padres, the Braves also beat the
                   Colorado Rockies 13 straight games in
                   1993
_ Question 242:   13
_ Question 243:   18
_ Question 244:   Michael Tucker
_ Question 245:   235

MISCELLANEOUS
_ Question 246:   Catcher
_ Question 247:   Joe Torre
_ Question 248:   Rafael Furcal
_ Question 249:   Dale Murphy
_ Question 250:   Tim Wakefield

Got your October total? Here's how it breaks down:

WALK-OFF BOMB TO WIN GAME 7 AND SERIES MVP HONORS	= 45-50
WON A RING IN A THRILLING SEVEN-GAME SERIES	= 40-44
GOOD JOB—YOU DID ENOUGH TO GET THE RING	= 35-39
LOST A TOUGH SEVEN-GAME SERIES	= 30-34
THEY'RE CALLING YOU THE "NEW" BILL BUCKNER	= 00-29

Think you can do better next season? Well, you're going to get a shot at it—Atlanta Braves IQ Volume II is coming in 2010!

About the Author

Tucker Elliot is a Georgia native and a diehard Braves fan. A former high school athletic director and varsity baseball coach, he now teaches journalism part time at a local college—but his fulltime job is volunteering at the local recreation league, coaching his son's little league team, chalking the fields, and working the concession stands.

References

WEBSITES
Baseball-reference.com
MLB.com
Atlanta.Braves.MLB.com
BaseballHallofFame.org
ESPN.com

BOOKS
Baseball, an Illustrated History, Geoffrey C. Ward and Ken Burns
The Team by Team Encyclopedia of Major League Baseball, Dennis Purdy
The Unofficial Guide to Baseball's Most Unusual Records, Bob Mackin
The 2005 ESPN Baseball Encyclopedia, edited by Pete Palmer and Gary Gillette
100 Years of the World Series, Eric Enders

Sports by the Numbers

The award-winning Sports by the Numbers book series is a proud sponsor of Black Mesa's IQ books. SBTN is the series where every number tells a story—and whether you're a beginning fan just learning the ropes, or a diehard fanatic hanging on the outcome of every game, the crew at SBTN have got you covered.

Check out Sports by the Numbers on the web:

www.sportsbythenumbers.com

Current titles include:

- *University of Oklahoma Football*
- *University of Georgia Football*
- *Major League Baseball*
- *New York Yankees*
- *Boston Red Sox*
- *San Francisco Giants*
- *Mixed Martial Arts*
- *NASCAR*

For information about special discounts for bulk purchases, please email:

sales@savasbeatie.com

Sports by the Numbers Praise

"You think you know it all? Not so fast. To unearth fact upon fact about this historic franchise in a unique yet tangible way is an impressive feat, which is why the following pages are more than worthwhile for every member of that cult known as Red Sox Nation . . . This is a book that Red Sox fans of all ages and types will enjoy and absorb."
  — Ian Browne, Boston Red Sox Beat Writer, MLB.com

"Fighting is physical storytelling where villains and heroes emerge, but the back-story is what makes the sport something that persisted from B.C. times to what we know it as today. Antonio Rodrigo Nogueira living through a childhood coma only to demonstrate equal grit inside the ring on his way to two world championships. Randy Couture defying age like it was as natural as sunrise on his way to six world championships. The achievements are endless in nature, but thanks to this book, these great human narratives are translated into a universal language—numbers—in a universal medium—fighting."
  — Danny Acosta, Sherdog.com and *Fight!* Magazine Writer

"Statistics have long been resigned to slower, contemplative sports. Finally, they get a crack at the world's fastest sport in this fascinating piece of MMA analysis."
  — Ben Zeidler, CagePotato.com, *Fight!* Magazine

"Long-time Sooner fans will revel in the flood of memories that flow from these pages. You'll think back to a defining moment—that favorite player, an afternoon next to the radio, or that special day at Owen Field. And the information contained here is so thorough that you'll relive those memories many times."
  — Bob Stoops, Head Coach, University of Oklahoma Football

"*University of Oklahoma Football – S*ports By The Numbers is a must read for all OU Football junkies. I read trivia I didn't know or had forgotten."
— Barry Switzer, Legendary Head Coach, University of Oklahoma Football

"Clever and insightful. For fans who don't know much about the history of stock-car racing, it's like taking the green flag."
— Monte Dutton, best-selling NASCAR author

"You will find the most important numbers that every fan should know, like Joe DiMaggio's 56-game hitting streak, Ted Williams' .406 batting average, Hank Aaron's 755 homeruns, and Nolan Ryan's seven no-hitters, but there are hundreds of lesser-known stats. Even if you think you know everything about baseball, I guarantee you will learn a whole lot from this book."
— Zack Hample, best-selling author of *Watching Baseball Smarter*

"This book is fascinating and informative. If you love Yankees trivia, this is the reference for you."
— Jane Heller, best-selling novelist, Yankees blogger, and author of *Confessions of a She-Fan: The Course of True Love with the New York Yankees*

"This book brings you tons of info on America's best loved and most hated team—the New York Yankees . . . a great book for any age or fan of America's Game and Team. A must read."
— Phil Speranza, author of the *2000 Yankee Encyclopedia 5th edition*

"The Yankees matter—but you already knew that, and soon, you will dive into this wonderful yield by the good folks at Sports by the Numbers and you will lose yourself in baseball, in history, in numbers, and in the New York Yankees. I envy you. I can't think

of a better way to pass the next couple of hours."
— Mike Vaccaro, best-selling author and award-winning columnist for the *New York Post*

"I loved this book. I could not put it down at night. This book is the perfect bedside or coffee table reading material. *New York Yankees: An Interactive Guide to the World of Sports* has a huge collection of interesting data about the entire New York Yankees history."
— Sam Hendricks, author of *Fantasy Football Guidebook* and *Fantasy Football Almanac 2009*

Black Mesa Titles

Look for these other titles in the IQ Series:

- *Mixed Martial Arts*
- *New York Yankees*
- *Boston Red Sox*
- *University of Oklahoma Football*
- *University of Georgia Football*

For information about special discounts for bulk purchases, please email:

black.mesa.publishing@gmail.com

Praise for MMA IQ

"Every time I work on a cut I am being tested and I feel confident I can pass the test. After reading MMA IQ I'm not so sure I can do the same with this book."
— UFC Cutman Jacob "Stitch" Duran,
www.stitchdurangear.com

"MMA fans everywhere pay attention—this is your best chance to reign supreme in your favorite bar stool. The trivia and stories come at you so fast and so furious you'll wish Stitch Duran was in your corner getting you ready to do battle."
— Sam Hendricks, award-winning author of *Fantasy Football Tips: 201 Ways to Win through Player Rankings, Cheat Sheets and Better Drafting*

"From the rookie fan to the pound for pound trivia champs, MMA IQ has something that will challenge the wide spectrum of fans that follow the sport."
— Robert Joyner, www.mmapayout.com

"I thought I knew MMA, but this book took my MMA IQ to a whole new level . . . fun read, highly recommended."
— William Li, www.findmmagym.com

You can visit *Mixed Martial Arts IQ* author Zac Robinson on the web:

www.sportsbythenumbersmma.com
www.cutmanstitchduran.com

Made in the USA
Lexington, KY
07 April 2010